Guest-edited by
DEBORAH SAUNT,
TOM GREENALL AND
ROBERTA MARCACCIO

The Business of Research

Knowledge and Learning Redefined in Architectural Practice

ARCHITECTURAL DESIGN
May/June 2019
Profile No 259

The Business of Research 03/2019

About the Guest-Editors
Deborah Saunt, Tom Greenall and Roberta Marcaccio
05

Introduction
Embracing Research in the Business of Architecture
Deborah Saunt, Tom Greenall and Roberta Marcaccio
06

Prologue
A Shared Practice
Anne Boddington
14

Resituated Research
Achieving Meaningful Impact on the Fault Line Between Academia and Practice
Harriet Harriss
18

Public Planning Reimagined
Building Capacity and Agency
Frederik Weissenborn
26

Practise What You Preach
The University as a Common Ground Between Research and its Application
Lara Kinneir
32

Aleks Stovjakovic, Wasteminster, London School of Architecture (LSA), 2016

Spanning Continuums
Addressing the Separation of Research and Practice in Architecture
Leon van Schaik
38

Out of Practice
Theoretical Speculations In and Out of the Business of Architecture
James Soane
48

Mitigation of Shock
Post-Occupancy Anthropology
Anab Jain, Jon Ardern and Danielle Knight
54

Siobhán Ní Éanaigh / McGarry Ní Éanaigh Architects, Coláiste Ailigh School, County Donegal, Ireland, 2013

How Is It For You?
Building Design as Experienced by Users and Makers
Ziona Strelitz
60

ISSN 0003-8504
ISBN 978 111 9546023

Guest-edited by **Deborah Saunt, Tom Greenall and Roberta Marcaccio**

OMA/AMO,
Prada Foundation,
Milan,
Italy,
2018

Vertically Integrated Research

An Unusual Business Model

Daniel Davis

68

Pushing the Envelope

Innovation and Collaboration at Bloomberg's New European Headquarters

Michael Jones

76

For the Public Good

Rebuilding the Architectural Profession's Social Contract

Rory Hyde

82

Research Infiltration

The Germination of Preoccupations

Carol Patterson

90

Deconstructing Research

A Reverse-Engineering Methodology and Practice

Alison Creba and Lionel Devlieger

96

Building Practices

The Infrastructure of Materials Research

Jane Hall

102

Translating Culture

Framing Indigenous Knowledge Through Architecture

Martyn Hook

108

Collective Impressions of Smithson Plaza

Weaving History with the Present

Deborah Saunt, Tom Greenall and Roberta Marcaccio

114

Assemble,
Goldsmiths Centre
for Contemporary Art,
New Cross,
London,
2018

Towards a New Normal

The Blurred Landscape of Architectural Research in China

John Zhang

120

Counterpoint

Less Grey, More Black and White

Architecture Needs a Consistent Platform in Research

David Green

126

Contributors

134

Editorial Offices
John Wiley & Sons
9600 Garsington Road
Oxford
OX4 2DQ

T +44 (0)1865 776868

Editor
Neil Spiller

Commissioning Editor
Helen Castle

Managing Editor
Caroline Ellerby
Caroline Ellerby Publishing

Freelance Contributing Editor
Abigail Grater

Publisher
Paul Sayer

Art Direction + Design
CHK Design:
Christian Küsters

Production Editor
Elizabeth Gongde

Prepress
Artmedia, London

Printed in Italy by Printer Trento Srl

Front cover: Graphics by Christian Küsters

Inside front cover: Leon van Schaik, Continuums ideogram, 2018. © Leon van Schaik

Page 1: DSDHA, Economist Plaza movement analysis, London, 2016. © DSDHA

Denise Bratton
Paul Brislin
Mark Burry
André Chaszar
Nigel Coates
Peter Cook
Teddy Cruz
Max Fordham
Massimiliano Fuksas
Kate Goodwin
Edwin Heathcote
Anthony Hunt
Charles Jencks
Bob Maxwell
Brian McGrath
Jayne Merkel
Peter Murray
Kester Rattenbury
Mark Robbins
Deborah Saunt
Patrik Schumacher
Coren Sharples
Neil Spiller
Leon van Schaik
Claire Weisz
Ken Yeang
Alejandro Zaera-Polo

EDITORIAL BOARD

△ ARCHITECTURAL DESIGN
May/June 2019
Profile No. 259

Disclaimer
The Publisher and Editors cannot be held responsible for errors or any consequences arising from the use of information contained in this journal; the views and opinions expressed do not necessarily reflect those of the Publisher and Editors, neither does the publication of advertisements constitute any endorsement by the Publisher and Editors of the products advertised.

Journal Customer Services
For ordering information, claims and any enquiry concerning your journal subscription please go to www.wileycustomerhelp.com/ask or contact your nearest office.

Americas
E: cs-journals@wiley.com
T: +1 781 388 8598 or
+1 800 835 6770 (toll free in the USA & Canada)

Europe, Middle East and Africa
E: cs-journals@wiley.com
T: +44 (0)1865 778315

Asia Pacific
E: cs-journals@wiley.com
T: +65 6511 8000

Japan (for Japanese-speaking support)
E: cs-japan@wiley.com
T: +65 6511 8010 or 005 316 50 480 (toll-free)

Visit our Online Customer Help available in 7 languages at www.wileycustomerhelp.com/ask

Print ISSN: 0003-8504
Online ISSN: 1554-2769

Prices are for six issues and include postage and handling charges. Individual-rate subscriptions must be paid by personal cheque or credit card. Individual-rate subscriptions may not be resold or used as library copies.

All prices are subject to change without notice.

Identification Statement
Periodicals Postage paid at Rahway, NJ 07065. Air freight and mailing in the USA by Mercury Media Processing, 1850 Elizabeth Avenue, Suite C, Rahway, NJ 07065, USA.

USA Postmaster
Please send address changes to *Architectural Design*, John Wiley & Sons Inc., c/o The Sheridan Press, PO Box 465, Hanover, PA 17331, USA

Rights and Permissions
Requests to the Publisher should be addressed to:
Permissions Department
John Wiley & Sons Ltd
The Atrium
Southern Gate
Chichester
West Sussex PO19 8SQ
UK

F: +44 (0)1243 770 620
E: Permissions@wiley.com

All Rights Reserved. No part of this publication may be reproduced, stored in a retrieval system or transmitted in any form or by any means, electronic, mechanical, photocopying, recording, scanning or otherwise, except under the terms of the Copyright, Designs and Patents Act 1988 or under the terms of a licence issued by the Copyright Licensing Agency Ltd, Barnard's Inn, 86 Fetter Lane, London EC4A 1EN, UK, without the permission in writing of the Publisher.

Subscribe to △
△ is published bimonthly and is available to purchase on both a subscription basis and as individual volumes at the following prices.

Prices
Individual copies:
£29.99 / US$45.00
Individual issues on
△ App for iPad:
£9.99 / US$13.99
Mailing fees for print may apply

Annual Subscription Rates
Student: £90 / US$137
print only
Personal: £136 / US$215
print and iPad access
Institutional: £310 / US$580
print or online
Institutional: £388 / US$725
combined print and online
6-issue subscription on
△ App for iPad: £44.99 / US$64.99

ABOUT THE GUEST-EDITORS

DEBORAH SAUNT, TOM GREENALL
AND ROBERTA MARCACCIO

Deborah Saunt, Roberta Marcaccio and Tom Greenall

Deborah Saunt, Tom Greenall and Roberta Marcaccio work together at London-based spatial design studio DSDHA, whose internationally acclaimed work is driven by research and spans architecture and the urban landscape as well as place-making. DSDHA was founded by Deborah with partner David Hills. She was later joined by Tom, now Associate Director, and then by Roberta, who came on board in 2015 as Head of Research and Communication.

Having carefully examined the role of research within DSDHA during her PhD as part of the RMIT University Research Programme, Deborah led the studio's formal evolution into a multidisciplinary team that delivers spatial strategies and bespoke designs, consistently tapping into the latent potential of each project to foster urban change. By adopting a people-centred approach, DSDHA deploys its spatial intelligence across a broad range of scales and urban contexts, always with the ethos that 'the city is our client'.

Recent examples of DSDHA's collaborations include the design and research carried out for the restoration of the Smithsons' Economist Plaza in London (see p 114–19 of this issue), as well as the development of time-based urban tactics to remodel a number of public spaces across the city so that they can better serve the changing needs of its users over time. In the past decade, the studio has twice been awarded the Royal Commission for the Exhibition of 1851's Research Fellowship in the Built Environment. The first research grant, in 2010, supported an intensive programme of investigations that led to the development of conceptual ideas for the Commission's legacy estate in South Kensington, which then eventually turned into a public-realm project for practice (currently under development). The second grant, in 2016, saw Tom, Roberta and other DSDHA members involved in a study of ways to better integrate cycling infrastructure into London's public spaces. Supervised by Deborah, this research was carried out in collaboration with Transport for London (TfL). The results have informed DSDHA's design methodology and are being tested on a range of new projects within the studio.

Alongside their work within DSDHA, Deborah, Tom and Roberta are deeply involved in teaching, and regularly write and lecture about architecture at institutions in both the UK and abroad. As well as being a trustee for the London School of Architecture (LSA), which she co-founded in 2015, Deborah currently runs a design studio at the University of Navarra in Spain. Since 2011 Tom has taught a design studio in the School of Architecture at the Royal College of Art (RCA), while Roberta has been teaching History and Theory of Architecture at the Architectural Association (AA) in London. ᗞ

Text © 2019 John Wiley & Sons Ltd. Image © DSDHA

EMBRACING RESEARCH IN THE BUSINESS OF ARCHITECTURE

INTRODUCTION

DEBORAH SAUNT, TOM GREENALL
AND ROBERTA MARCACCIO

Cover of △ What about Learning, May 1968

Edited by Monica Pidgeon and Robin Middleton, and guest-edited by Cedric Price, the issue also included contributions by Peter Cook and Norman Foster, among others. Throughout his career, Price defended the renewal of architectural education in the UK and elsewhere, promoting the blurring between theoretical and professional realms and the idea of a project as an educational tool.

'Research' is the new buzzword. A quick survey of architects' websites around the world will show that the term features prominently among the range of services offered by contemporary practices. Professional institutions on both sides of the Atlantic also agree on the centrality of research, with the Royal Institute of British Architects (RIBA) aiming to 'facilitate collaboration, research and innovation in practice'[1] and the American Institute of Architects (AIA) declaring that 'empowering architects to use and engage in research' is fundamental to its mission.[2] This emphasis on research as an integral part of practice is indicative of a recent shift. Traditionally thought of as the domain of universities, with its value measured by the number of citations a paper/thesis received by fellow academics, today, and often, architectural research inhabits a grey area between academia and practice.

On the one hand, shifting funding models, globalisation and digital media have been forcing academia to question its scope and modes of evaluation of research, while on the other a wave of practitioners and new types of institutions, such as RMIT University in Melbourne or the London School of Architecture (LSA), have been recasting architectural education and theoretical speculation within practice. In so doing they have turned the traditional architectural studio into a learning environment that adopts and adapts academic models, and – more or less explicitly – posits architectural research as an end in itself as well as a potential source of business intelligence – as a means to self-generate future commissions and speculative opportunities that sometimes even shift the terrain of practice.

These modes of working seek to destabilise traditional roles of academia and practice by questioning their deep-rooted separation and demanding a new definition of the term 'research', one that is relevant to both parties as well as to the wider public. These are urgent issues to debate, particularly as, while both agree upon its centrality, there seems to be no consensus as to what effectively constitutes research, nor is there agreement on how its outcomes are to be assessed outside of codified academic systems.

In order to understand what form(s) and value(s) research assumes in this emerging landscape, this edition of ⌂ gathers together contributions from international scholars, researchers and from a number of practitioners who have been recasting intellectual speculation and learning within their own studios. These considerations advance a series of hypotheses on the value of research beyond a purely academic context, and on how academia could participate in the contemporary cultural shifts happening within practice, while also raising questions in terms of opportunities and risks that arise when research is recast into the less regimented realm of practice.

Changes in Academia / Practice / Economy

In the UK, research has been central to the academic system since at least the 19th century, when architecture, once largely taught by pupillage (paid or unpaid internships in offices supplemented by private courses) officially entered the physical and institutional space of the university, while progressively distancing itself from practice. The divorce was sanctioned in 1958, when the RIBA's Oxford Conference of Architectural Education, held at the university's Magdalen

DSDHA,
The Business of Research Symposium,
Foster + Partners,
London,
July 2017

In preparation for this issue of ⌂, DSDHA invited some of the contributors to meet and discuss the emerging landscape of practice-based architectural research. From left to right: Irene Gallou (Foster + Partners), Ziona Strelitz (ZZA Responsive User Environments), Daniel Davis (WeWork), Frederik Weissenborn (Public Practice) and Shumi Bose (RIBA/Central Saint Martins).

College, virtually banished apprenticeship in practice in an attempt to develop a more rigorous research agenda that would map onto university expectations. Since then, architectural research within academia has been understood as a form of theoretical and critical inquiry, to be carried out in any architectural domain (from technology and construction to design, history and theory) and relying on a scientific methodology and the activities of collecting, organising and presenting/sharing information (usually in the form of a thesis/argument), but often with little effort being made to reach out beyond the academic system to impact on work in practice, for instance.

School of Architecture,
Ashton Street,
University of Liverpool,
in 1920

The first school of architecture in a university was established at the Massachusetts Institute of Technology (MIT) in Boston, Massachusetts, and opened as a department within the school of Industrial Science in 1866. Other schools, like the Liverpool School of Architecture pictured here, which was the first to run RIBA-accredited degrees in architecture from 1902, were then established in the US and Europe following its model, with classrooms and drawing rooms organised around a collection of photographs, models, decorative materials and books considered as important forms of instruction.

More recently, cuts in government funding for higher education and new societal concerns have been forcing universities to run on the for-profit model of the business corporation, with the production of fundable research being central to their branding and financial viability. For example, the Royal College of Art (RCA) and British Land (one of the largest property development and investment companies in the UK) have recently started a design partnership to 'challenge students to find creative solutions to development opportunities across British Land's portfolio',[3] while Columbia University Graduate School of Architecture, Planning and Preservation (GSAPP) joined forces with Audi to 'develop and test new paradigms in the relationship between motion, mobility and design'.[4]

Architects, on the other hand, have been confronting a 'crisis of relevance'. This is due to difficulties in communicating with a public that has little understanding of what architects actually do, and thus struggles to recognise how their work creates value (though this is true also within the profession itself). Architecture is indeed often predicated on the misconception that architects only make buildings. In reality, architectural design services account for a rather small percentage of a project's total capital cost, with construction typically involving an entire army of other specialists: from contractors to project managers, development managers, masterplanners, and a rainbow spectrum of engineers, interior designers and so on. The more complex construction technology becomes, the more architects' authority is diminished and, as a consequence, their role marginalised within society – a trend that can only escalate with AI and parametric design threatening to further automate construction processes.

To respond to this crisis, architects have had to step up their game. Not only have they had to abandon the long-standing myth that 'doing architecture through the act of design is a form of research in its own right',[5] but also traditional practice-based research activities, such as background-gathering of site data, material studies, context analysis or basic post-occupancy evaluation have been required to reach higher levels of sophistication. To achieve this, practitioners have sought collaborations with academics, as well as building in-house the skills/resources to better access alternative and external funding streams. DSDHA, for instance, has received two generous grants from the Royal Commission for the Exhibition of 1851 to investigate pressing urban issues.

Cover of *A Right to Build*, University of Sheffield School of Architecture and Architecture 00:/, 2011

The publication is the result of a Knowledge Transfer research collaboration between the University of Sheffield School of Architecture and the practice Architecture 00:/ to propose possible solutions to the current housing crisis.

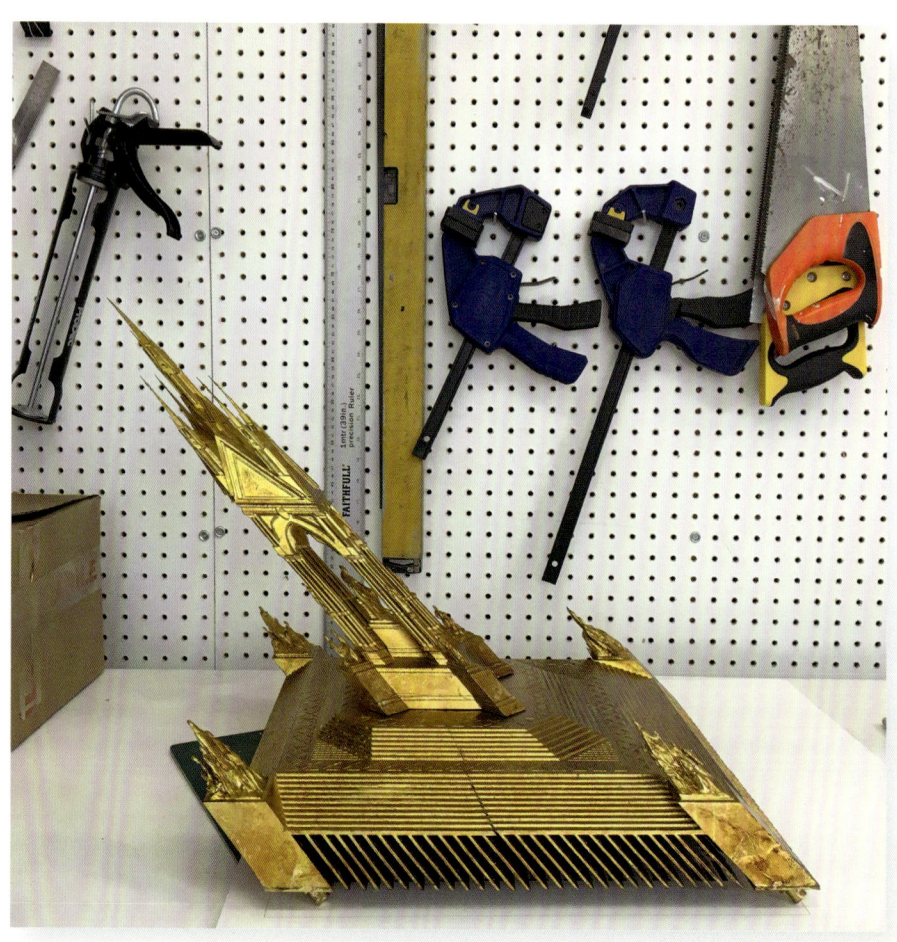

DSDHA, Distorted model of the Albert Memorial, London, 2017

The model is the result of the in-depth investigations undertaken by DSDHA as part of the 2010 Research Fellowship in the Built Environment, awarded to the practice by the Royal Commission for the Exhibition of 1851 to study and draw a long-term vision for its estate in South Kensington.

DSDHA,
Snapshot from a visual sequence analysing the experience of moving through London as a cyclist,
2018

In 2016 DSDHA was awarded a second Research Fellowship in the Built Environment by the Royal Commission for the Exhibition of 1851 to look at how cycling can best be integrated in London's historic core while the city continues to shift away from the prominence of car use. Having considered often-overlooked aspects of aesthetic and psychological order, DSDHA have developed a methodology for the appraisal of existing schemes and the design of shared junctions that integrate cycling and walking with other modes of transportation.

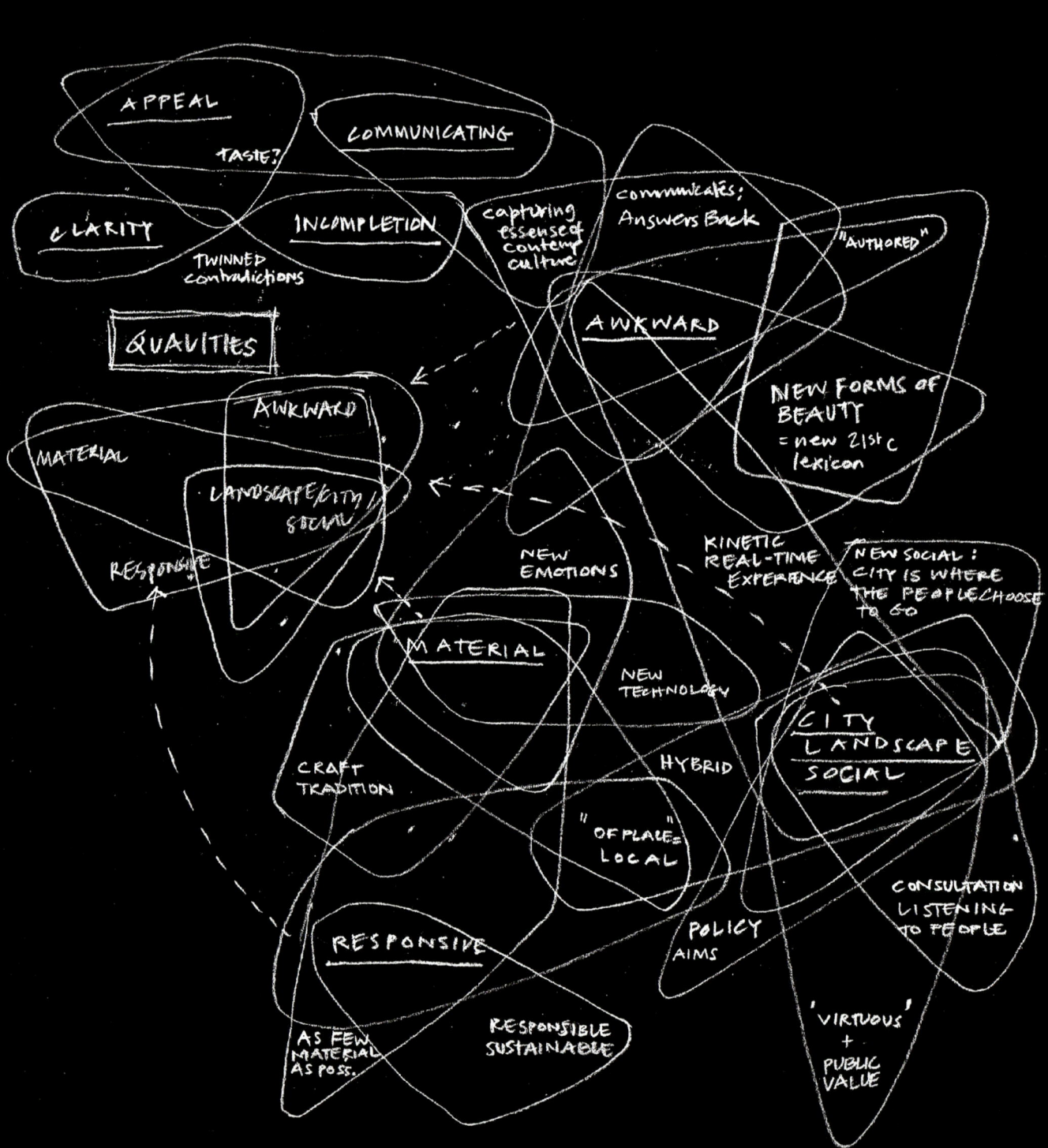

RMIT University has introduced a radical programme to bridge the chasm between academia and practice, and award PhDs to practitioners keen to thoroughly investigate their own modes of working

DSDHA design process, 2010

Through her PhD at RMIT University in Melbourne, DSDHA Director Deborah Saunt recognised research as one of the most valuable productions of her practice. Since then DSDHA has set up a separate studio offering 'spatial strategies' and research as independent services, to redefine the practice's relevance in relation to contemporary needs and to enhance the long-term resilience of the business.

Academia Versus Practice
In this sense, the new emphasis on research is not just a way to benefit from R&D tax breaks or be more competitive by offering an additional professional service; it is a sign of a profession in the midst of redefining itself, striving to bring into focus its relevance, agency and advocacy to society as well as to make itself resilient within the so-called 'knowledge economy'.

To help architects in this endeavour, as Leon van Schaik discusses in his article in this issue of ⌾ (pp 38–47), RMIT University has introduced a radical programme to bridge the chasm between academia and practice, and award PhDs to practitioners keen to thoroughly investigate their own modes of working. The school has been able to demonstrate that those who have taken this path have become more likely to win competitions and enjoy an enhanced reputation.

Largely inspired by RMIT, the recently founded LSA relies on a network of London-based practices who supply financial and academic support, and employ salaried students on a part-time basis, to create a cost-neutral educational model. Crucially, this model is not just about educational reform; it also seeks to restructure practice, encouraging professionals to teach and participate in the school's research in order to stimulate in practice the type of rigorous intellectual speculation and radical ambition that architectural education should foster.

While Harriet Harriss's contribution to the issue (pp 18–25) draws a comprehensive outline of the current state of architectural education and research with a particular focus on the UK, John Zhang (pp 120–25) takes us to China, where schools are involved in making buildings; developers undertake independent research and architects work on a 'thesis' rather than on 'projects'. He warns us of some of the potential dangers of blending practice and academia.

Dissemination: Publish or Perish
Harriss also suggests taking the LSA's research-led approach to education further, allowing architectural studios to offer research degrees to salaried academics through placements within practices. This in turn might stimulate professionals to share the knowledge they produce within their studios, something practices are typically quite protective of. Anne Boddington (pp 14–17) highlights that practice-based research currently lacks the effective channels of dissemination as well as the rigorous process of scrutiny enjoyed by academic research, and remarks that sharing research, no matter whether it is produced within practice or academia, is an ethical issue for the profession as a whole.

It is no coincidence therefore that to revitalise the planning sector, Public Practice (pp 26–31) has placed a cohort of 'associates' in different planning departments across London who dedicate 10 per cent of their time to collective research, overseen by Public Practice and allowing them to develop critical skills and knowhow which can then be transmitted to their host authority and shared across the planning sector.

Rory Hyde even goes as far as to suggest that a 'democratised version of the data-driven approach' to design might be key to unlocking the knowledge generated by individual practices, which currently lives as isolated chunks on individual servers (see his article on pp 82–9). For him, creating a giant knowledge base that all practitioners could draw from would allow practices to learn from each other's successes and mistakes to meet architecture's obligations towards society, rather than just for the benefit of individual clients.

The issue of dissemination is also central to James Soane's critique of the RIBA's continuing professional development (CPD) curriculum, a compulsory series of courses for all architects in practice, which excludes critical reflection and focuses instead on technical knowhow (pp 48–53). In response, his research-led studio Project Orange asked each member of staff to research and write up an area of personal interest with reference to projects in the office. This exercise allowed them to share their experiences internally as well as to formulate a hypothesis on how their collective critical position could contribute to contemporary architectural theory.

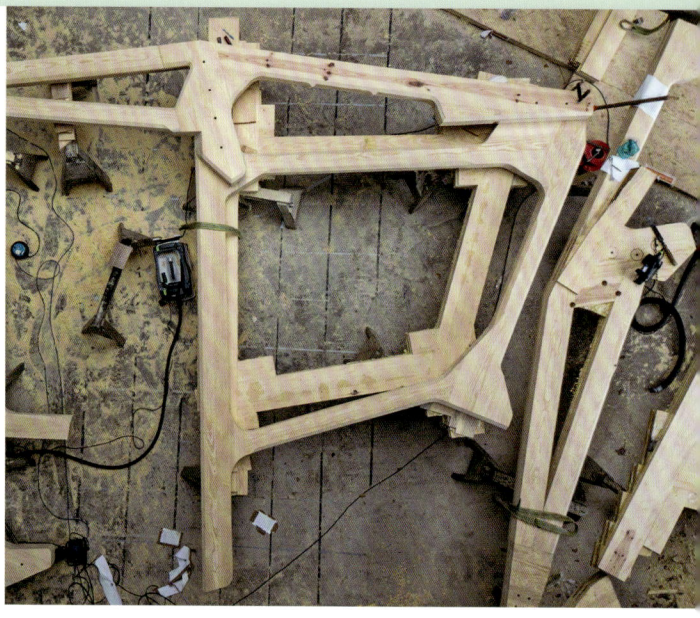

Architectural Association (AA),
Wakeford Hall Library Phase 1,
Hooke Park campus,
Beaminster, Dorset, UK,
2017

Components for the design of a library space, formed from a series of planar frames. The frames are a homemade cross-laminated timber/Glulam hybrid, glued together in the workshop and then sculpted with a five-axis robotic arm. As an example of collaboration between practitioners and an academic institution, the frame was designed by AA students helped by Arup engineers Adam Buchanan, Tara Clinton and Francis Archer.

Architectural Association (AA), Sawmill Shelter,
Hooke Park campus,
Beaminster, Dorset, UK,
2017

The timber canopy was designed by AA students and engineered by Arup (Vincenzo Reale, Francis Archer and Conor Hayes). Investigating the limits of timber in tension, the shelter is a test-bed for the prototyping of structural systems that will be deployed in the next planned construction at Hooke Park.

Practitioners have sought collaborations with academics, as well as building in-house the skills/resources to better access alternative and external funding streams

Research into Business Strategy

For some practices, research can become self-sustaining if offered as an independent service, like Ziona Strelitz's ZZA Responsive User Environments consultancy for instance (pp 60–67), which conducts user-focused research and post-occupancy evaluation on behalf of architects or their clients. While this is something that neither architects nor their professional bodies appear to ascribe much business benefit to (as demonstrated by the fact that post-occupancy evaluation sits at the bottom of the RIBA Plan of Work as a non-compulsory stage of the design that bears little or no relation to the linear process that precedes it), for her this type of research has to be strictly carried out independently of the design process in order to produce meaningful insights.

This is in sharp contrast with WeWork's business model, which according to Director of Research Daniel Davis (pp 68–75) offers an opportunity for carrying out research that has not been historically possible in either academia or unintegrated architectural practices. The research team at WeWork continuously monitors the performance of their extensive property portfolio, using a form of 'soft AI' to help understand what makes one office more successful than another. This then informs future designs as well as their business strategy.

Some practices use research to build or consolidate a reputation in a particular sector, for example Foster + Partners at the forefront of environmental performance and control, deploying empirical methods to test the performance of their design proposals (pp 76–81). Others use research to venture into different disciplinary territories, as in the case of AMO, an independent research branch established to expand OMA's remit into the realm of media, fashion and communication to get back a share of practice that had been lost to consultancies in the late 1990s and early 2000s (pp 90–95). Similarly, the Belgian-based collective Rotor (pp 96–101) has used 'interdisciplinary research' to establish an alternative type of practice, blurring the boundaries between academic research and business consultancy, with the aim of developing sustainable, witty and viable solutions to reuse the sheer volume of waste material generated by construction and demolition processes within architecture.

Past / Present / Future

A crucial point raised by Daniel Davis's article has to do with time: architecture is a peculiar profession, obsessed with its remote past (students study the Pyramids and Ancient Greek architecture) and concerned with a distant future (if we were unable to convince clients that the future will be radically different, we would be out of work), yet somewhat struggling to look at the present/its immediate past, which is precisely what WeWork's research unit does.

By contrast, iredale pedersen hook's and DSDHA's case studies (pp 108–13 and 114–19) show to what extent historical research is key, alongside consultation and 'grounded research' to understand the present situation and devise spatial strategies for either contested sites such as Yagan Square in Perth, Western Australia, or historically significant ones like the Smithsons' Economist Plaza in London. On the other hand, Superflux (pp 54–9) believe that speculating on the future is essential in order for architects to be able to claim back their agency and act upon the present. As a studio they research and build 1:1 immersive scenarios through which they show the public what our lives might be like in a distant future, if for instance we do nothing to combat global warming. The ultimate goal of these fictional settings is to have an impact on people's understanding of reality and shape future policies, decisions and behaviours.

Turning Answers into Questions

All the case studies in the issue show a range of attempts from practices of all sizes to move away from more canonical forms of research towards more sophisticated ways of framing their methods of investigation and outputs. Jane Hall's text (pp 102–7) is perhaps the most explicit in declaring this as the very intent of the multidisciplinary collective Assemble. As they grew in scale and departed from self-constructed projects, having to delegate construction process to a third party, the studio had to translate its original mantra of 'doing things ourselves' into 'materials research', adapting both their social and spatial infrastructures to maintain a collaborative, hands-on method of working.

Together, the contributions to this 𝐷 call for a revision of the idea that context analysis, a design methodology and vocational training are the sole skills needed by practitioners, while a higher level of knowledge expansion, – a licence to contribute to the wider disciplinary discourse – is the prerogative of professors/academics. In contrast to this binary definition, the issue reveals that the most valuable research, whether it is subsidised or self-funded, independent from the project or integral to it, is that which successfully structures a dialogue between different audiences: speaking the language of practitioners as well as academics, engaging clients, the public sector and the general public alike, allowing each party to question assumptions and together evolve the disciplinary discourse. This type of research acknowledges that good architecture requires multi-headed teams with specialisms in different fields who have discovered ways to work collaboratively, with or without the aid of technology, and to share authorship. 𝐷

Notes
1. www.architecture.com/about/riba-board/open-call-for-vice-president-research-2018-2019.
2. www.aia.org/pages/5626-architectural-research.
3 'British Land Announces Three-Year Partnership with the Royal College of Art', 27 July 2016: www.britishland.com/news-and-views/press-releases/2016/27-07-2016b.
4. http://www.experimentsinmotion.com/about/.
5. Reinier de Graaf, in *Volume* #48: *The Research Turn*, May 2016.

Text © 2019 John Wiley & Sons Ltd. Images: p 7(t) © Foster + Partners; p 7(b) © RIBA Collections; p 8(t) Courtesy of Architecture 00/; pp 8(b), 9-10 DSDHA; p 12(t) Photo by Aitor Almaraz, courtesy of ARUP; p 12(b) Photo by Vincenzo Reale, courtesy of ARUP

Anne Boddington

A. Producing culture on the bus
B. Play culture in a gaming arena
C. Performance & watching informal theatre
D. Production and maker spaces
E. Night time culture in the Underground
F. Orchestra performance & making music
G. Consuming culture on Crossrail
H. Dance rehearsal & Art class

PROLOGUE

A SHARED PRACTICE

Architectural research is of little value in isolation: it should serve to broaden and deepen the knowledge base of the profession. **Anne Boddington** – chair of the art and design sub-panel of the Research Excellence Framework, which assesses research quality in UK higher-education institutions – considers how this can be achieved by breaking boundaries both within practice itself and between practice and academia, including through newly instated graduate apprenticeships.

DSDHA and the London School of Architecture (LSA),
Integration of cultural uses within new
and existing transport infrastructure,
Whitechapel, London,
2017

Working collaboratively with their students from the LSA's Metabolic City Design Think Tank (Louie Austen, Charlotte Hurley, Molly Judge, Lloyd Martin and Sheenwar Siti), DSDHA have addressed some of the issues raised by the Mayor's Cultural Infrastructure Plan and devised a citywide spatial strategy that operates between mobility and public space to create much-needed sites for informal cultural participation and production.

The (re-)introduction of graduate apprenticeships to the landscape of architectural education in 2018 represents a watershed moment, as practices may once again now opt to take on and accept responsibility for educating and training the next generations of architects. The implications of these changes in the relationships, dialogue and 'duty of care' for our professional bodies, for our regulators, for architectural practice and for higher education are significant as the responsibilities and expertise of each are repositioned. Providing less debt-ridden options for future students alters the historical status quo and suggests new and different roles for all. It also signals a collective need to recognise, respect and harness existing forms of knowledge and skills in new ways. For the first time, the craft of architectural education will be tested and regulated in architectural practice. Practitioners will be required to professionally educate as well as to educate professionally. But what of the 'business of research' in such a context?

A number of contributors to this issue of △ describe how and what 'research' is conducted and integrated in the business models of architectural practice, and the enrichment and added-value it brings to the production and/or evaluation of built work. This 'research' is undoubtedly of significant value to those practices and their production, but how is it systematically translated, shared with others and captured for future generations? How does the architectural profession learn, advance and enhance the quality of architecture and the public realm through a collaborative dialogue?

The Research Excellence Framework, the system for assessing the quality of research in the UK's higher-education institutions, defines research as: 'a process of investigation leading to new insights, effectively shared'. This is a generous definition in outlining knowledge development, but critically requires that knowledge from research is accessible to others and can inform and advance – in this case – architectural knowledge and all modes of its production.

> Given the changing nature of architectural education, including the reintroduction of graduate apprenticeships and the expansion of research in practice, there is an imperative for a new strategic dialogue

Jeremy Till's elegantly concise articulation of architectural research, commissioned by the Royal Institute of British Architects (RIBA) in 2007,[1] and Harriet Harriss's and Rory Hyde's essays in this issue (pp 18–25 and 82–9), each in their different ways, press for the democratisation and diversification of architectural research futures, although to whom and how such conversations are facilitated remains unclear. How can professionals and researchers take collective responsibility for 'open access' to their research and its contribution to the development of architectural knowledge? Consensus as to a working definition of research would be a first and helpful step forward, particularly as there are still significant gaps in our inter- and intra-professional dialogue and understanding, in our willingness and capacity to 'share' knowledge and facilitate professional learning, and inconsistency in teaching the rigour and competencies of research practice. Designation of research as a core professional competency might also serve to resolve a longstanding pedagogic challenge, where research is generally perceived as the remit of academics and of limited 'value' to practice.

Given the changing nature of architectural education, including the reintroduction of graduate apprenticeships and the expansion of research in practice, there is an imperative for a new strategic dialogue. Professional expectations and responsibilities need to be revisited, and the changing relationships between architectural practice and higher education re-examined to reposition and value the expertise we all bring to our diverse profession. Sharing research is possible, as is integrating teaching, research and research skills within architectural practice if there is a collective will to do so. But it requires all parties to learn new ways of working together and towards common goals. Research is by definition a shared practice; it is not a practice confined to individual or localised endeavour, but about a wider contribution to architectural knowledge. It is our professional responsibility to ensure that we support future generations of architects and architectural researchers in practice and in higher education, by giving them agency and ensuring they can contribute to informing the quality of the buildings, cities and landscapes they occupy. ᗭ

Note
1. First published as Jeremy Till, 'Three Myths and One Model', *Building Material*, 17, 2008, pp 4–10; https://jeremytill.s3.amazonaws.com/uploads/post/attachment/34/2007_Three_Myths_and_One_Model.pdf.

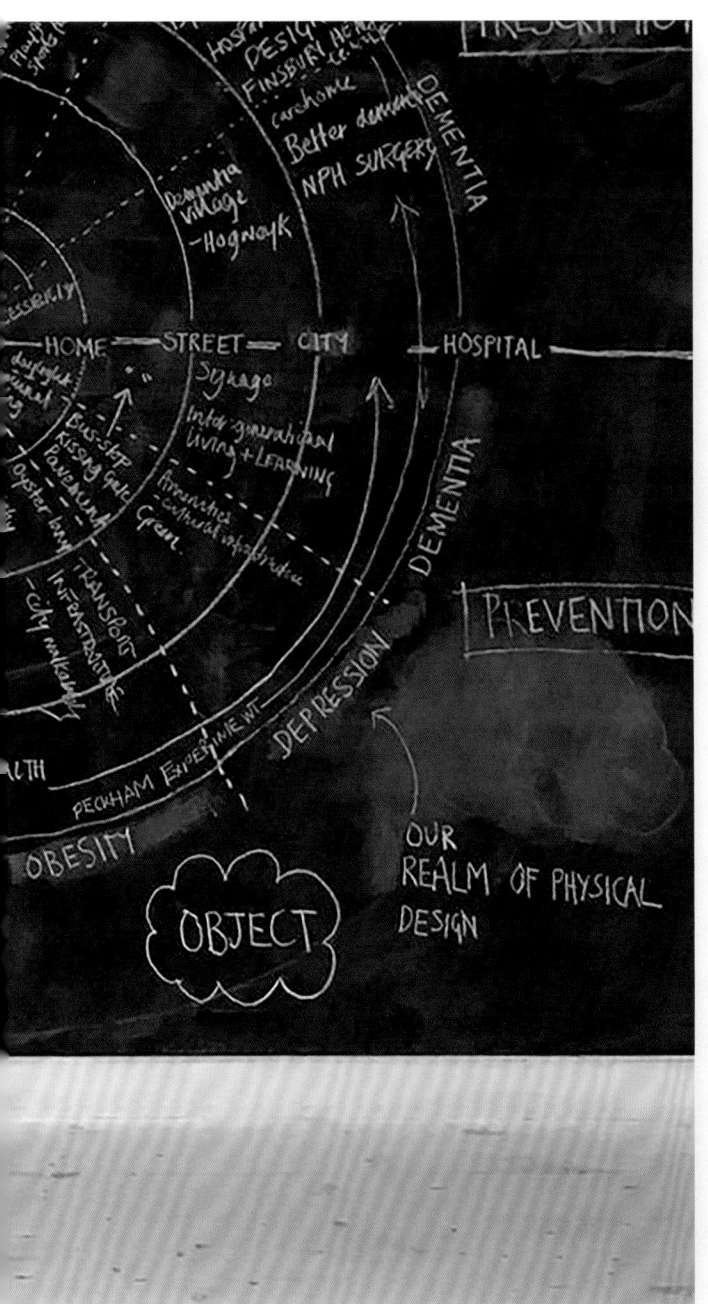

A student working on a design proposal to challenge the identity of London, London School of Architecture (LSA), London, 2016

The LSA's postgraduate programme was founded in 2015 to offer an alternative route through the profession, providing an answer to the crisis affecting contemporary British education, which was accused of being expensive and out of touch with the realities of working in practice. The LSA is supported by the Practice Network – a community of 100 London practices who provide work placements, teaching and physical resources (meeting- and classrooms, computers, printing facilities). In order to remain 'cost neutral' for the students, the school does not have an institutional base. Instead it 'plugs' into existing institutions and practices, making the most of underused resources across London – a library here, a lecture theatre there – to test different modes of collaboration.

Text © 2019 John Wiley & Sons Ltd. Images: pp 14–15 © DSDHA; pp 16–17 Courtesy of LSA

RESITUATED RESEARCH

Harriet Harriss

ACHIEVING MEANINGFUL IMPACT ON THE FAULT LINE BETWEEN ACADEMIA AND PRACTICE

Kamil Dalkir,
Collective Equipment,
Objects / Bodies / Territories,
School of Architecture,
Royal College of Art (RCA),
London, 2016

The Objects / Bodies / Territories research project traced the impact of the Syrian migrant crisis on the sociopolitical as well as physical landscape of the Greek island of Lesbos. The island is a critical point on the journey from Syria to Europe, where the displacement of people has given rise to the displacement of architecture. The models here reproduce the architectures, infrastructure and objects that have been used, created or modified by the displaced in Lesbos.

The traditionally institutionalised nature of research can limit its practical relevance and the diversity of individuals involved in it. Practice-based PhDs are an increasingly popular way of addressing these issues. **Harriet Harriss**, who leads the Architecture Research Programme at London's Royal College of Art and is a member of the UK Department for Education construction industry panel, outlines their multiple benefits in terms of both student affordability and enhancement of the profession.

Should academic research impact upon architectural practice? Given there are 51 Royal Institute of British Architects (RIBA)-validated schools of architecture in the UK actively generating research, it is only reasonable for an architect to assume so. Whether or not it does is another matter. What also matters is that the academic environment is changing and there are a myriad of perspectives on the consequences of these changes that swing pendulously between the dystopian and desirable. It may, therefore, take a critical if consciously oversimplified analysis of the current situation to help identify the problems as well as the opportunities offered by academic research, particularly for forward-thinking practices.

Research is a product of its context *and* a product of its producers. In the face of ongoing political, socioeconomic and technological uncertainty both within and beyond the sector, the question we must now consider is whether research is best situated in academe by default, or whether resituating it in architecture practices could yield more tangible and transformative outcomes.

Research for Whom?
Despite the privatisation of higher education in the UK,[1] and perhaps because of it, universities, quite rightly, face increasing scrutiny over whose interests their research serves. Non-commercial funding bodies such as charities, commissions, national councils and government departments are assumed to be interested in research that results in palpable social and economic benefits to society. In contrast, 'commercial' research, undertaken by private, national and international businesses, external sponsors and corporations is often suspiciously presupposed to direct research towards achieving demonstrable impact upon their own organisation, and more often than not only focuses on outcomes that will increase their performance and profitability.

For some commentators, any funding criterion requiring predetermined outcomes (regardless of its public or private pedigree) only serves to corrode academic integrity, freedom and focus, and it is only unfettered, curiosity-driven experimental research that can either invent (an entirely new idea) or innovate (repurpose an existing idea). Of course, it is never strictly this binary. 'Unfettered' research can be just as self-indulgent as commercial research, if the rise in auto-ethnographic (self-as-subject) enquiry is anything to go by,[2] and governmental departments can be just as inclined as commercial sponsors to expect outcomes that advance their policies and reinforce their view of the world.[3] Subsequently, funding bids encumbered with predetermined outcomes seldom offer a Trojan-horse-style challenge to power. Instead, there is little freedom of thought or freedom from finance in academe.

Research by Whom?
Recent developments such as #MeToo, the Race Disparity Audit, the decolonisation of the curriculum movement and gender pay gap reporting have highlighted persistent inequalities across a range of sectors. In response, the UK's Research and Innovation organisation, set up in April 2018 to forge research partnerships between universities, businesses, charities and other research agencies, has established an external advisory group that has pledged to improve equality, diversity and inclusion right across the research and innovation landscape,[4] although how this will happen is not yet clear. Figures published by the Higher Education Statistics Agency (HESA) in 2017 recorded 'no black academics in the elite staff category of managers, directors and senior officials',[5] whereas the number of female professorial appointments is in decline despite the fact that only a quarter of UK professors are women.[6] Why this matters is because research activity – in terms of freedom, focus and finance – increases exponentially with rank, leaving white men better positioned to produce research and to provide the benchmark against which their colleagues' research performance is judged. It also means having the unrivalled ability to determine who and what is a worthy subject for research. As a direct consequence, the needs of vast sections of the population are simply ignored by research, which serves to reinforce public perception (and potential reality) that the research pursuits of academe are largely irrelevant to them.

Irrelevant Research?
Despite the fact that approximately 2.5 million academic papers are published each year,[7] only a few seem to have positively impacted upon the world's problems generally or architectural production specifically. In academe, 'impact' is often measured by how many times an architectural research paper is cited rather than the number of spatial outcomes it has generated. The tendency towards the use of academic-ese does not help to make impact statements easy reading, and often reinforces the view that academic

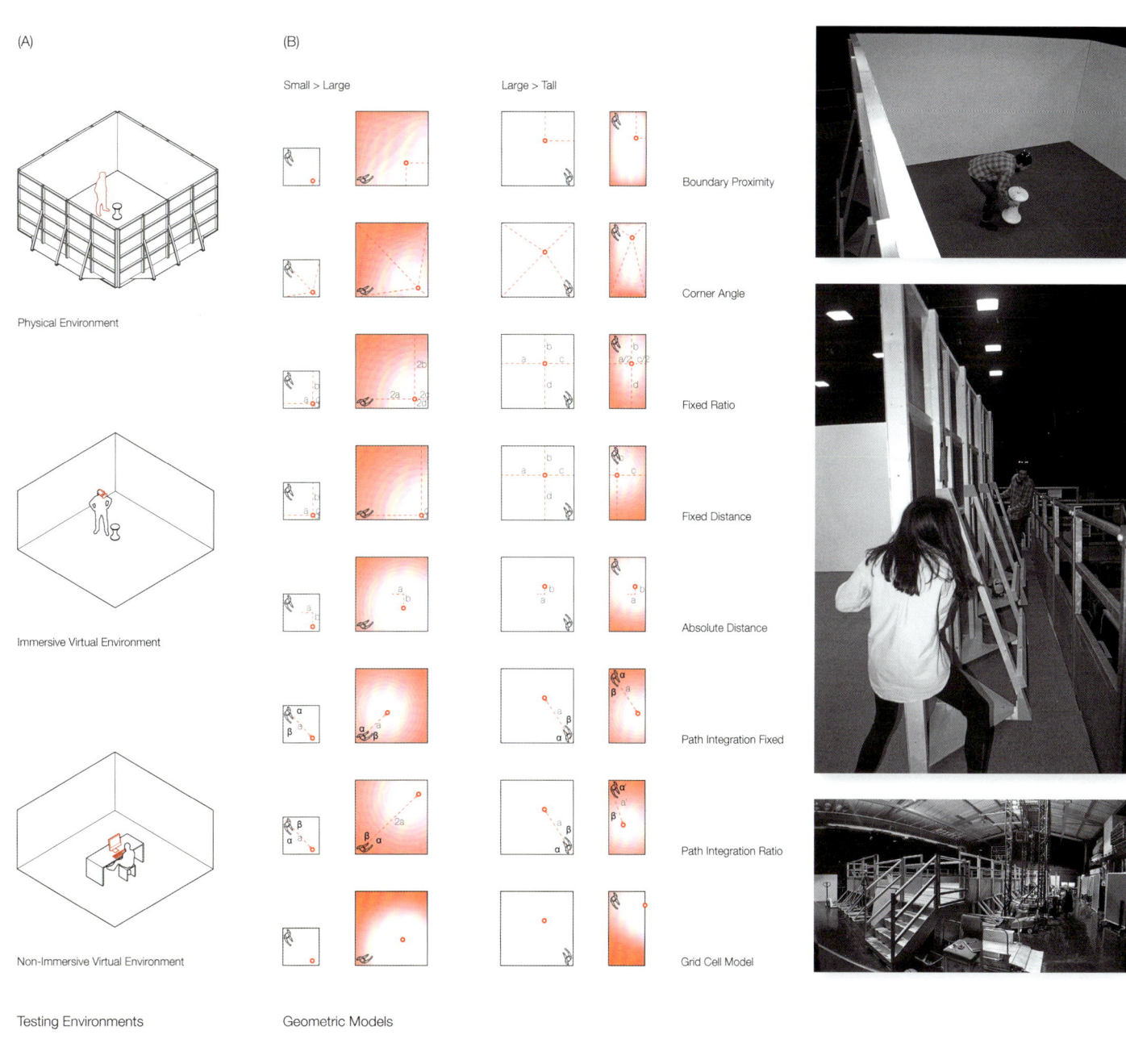

Fiona Zisch,
Distorting Space,
Bartlett School of Architecture and
the Institute of Behavioural Neuroscience,
University College London (UCL),
2017-18

Working across disciplines towards an informed conversation between architecture and cognitive neuroscience, Zisch's work explores cognitive mapping, human perception and architecture. She uses physical and virtual spaces and a range of digital technologies to map and understand movement in space and in the brain. The diagrams and photographs show a series of experiments investigating the impact of geometric changes on spatial memory in both physical and virtual-reality spaces.

Despite the fact that approximately 2.5 million academic papers are published each year, only a few seem to have positively impacted upon the world's problems generally or architectural production specifically research is largely intended for academic vindication rather than public value. Perhaps this explains the gulf of opinion between scientists and the general public on a range of issues. In one example, only 65 per cent of the American public compared to 98 per cent of scientists think humans are an evolved species.[8] Evidently, what needs to evolve is how academic research can be made more widely accessible and practically usable. Otherwise, the problem of irrelevance will only persist.

Architectural Research in Science and the Humanities
The lack of consensus over what constitutes architectural research is mirrored by the lack of consensus over what architectural practice actually involves. Before migrating to universities, architecture was taught by master builders on site then later in building colleges, and viewed as a vocation rather than a discipline. At only 200 years old, it remains a relatively modern invention in academic terms. As disciplinary newcomers, lasciviously traversing the five established epistemologies was inevitable if not intentional,[9] and allowed architecture to wet-nurse from an intoxicating and often at-odds range of surrogates including the 'natural sciences' (physics), the 'formal sciences' (statistics and systems science), the humanities (visual arts and philosophy), the social sciences (anthropology, sociology, psychology, geography, politics, economics) and the 'professional and applied sciences' (education, environment, media and business). This form of epistemological co-parenting has entitled architectural research to situate itself as a humanities subject and a science subject able to utilise methodologies aligned with both kinds of enquiry. Yet despite this, architecture is often positioned as a subcategory in research funding eligibility and forced to compete against its more sagacious epistemological ancestors for increasingly limited funds. However, if architectural research were to recognise its disciplinary hybridity as a facilitator rather than a fault line, leveraging this uniqueness could be one route to reasserting its relevance.

Architecture is often positioned as a subcategory in research funding eligibility and forced to compete against its more sagacious epistemological ancestors for increasingly limited funds

Practical Academic Research
Doctoral education is going through a period of transition. An increasing number of architecture schools are moving beyond the traditional by-thesis PhD model and offering practice-based and practice-led doctorates, although the two are often confused and conflated. Whereas a by-thesis doctorate typically offers researchers the chance to interrogate history and generate theory from the relative comfort of an archive, practice-based study (also known as a professional PhD) offers students or practitioners the chance to conduct an equally rigorous study into an aspect of architectural practice, can take place in an architectural office and can result in all kinds of business-enhancing outcomes.

In contrast, practice-led research (sometimes referred to as by-practice research) can use creative outcomes, from designs, models and buildings to digital tools, policy papers and media platforms as part of its claim of originality and contribution to knowledge, alongside a body of written text aimed at supporting these claims. This differs from practice-based study whereby the creative elements (such as the design of buildings) can be described but not submitted as part of the outcome. The transition towards more practical architectural research evidently offers under-leveraged benefits to architectural practice. Not only do practice-based PhDs open up more affordable routes to qualification (given the average cost of a PhD is around £200,000 for four years' full-time study in the UK), there is every possibility that this proximity to practice will increase the likely relevance and impact of architectural research. Where such research is limited, however, is due to its localised nature. Meta-questions with sector-wide and even global implications are sometimes difficult to ask when researchers are deeply embedded within a single-practice context. But in a period where few architecture practices can afford to resource their own research and development (R&D) departments, practice-based PhDs can offer the means through which businesses can find ways to advance their expertise, develop their IP and assert their USP for the cost of a single salary.

De-institutionalised Research, Public Trust and Architecture's Value
Although a recent study identified that a PhD offers no guarantee of a higher salary than a Master's-level qualification,[10] universities happily welcome the rising number of PhD candidates due to the increase in income they offer. However, the real value of architectural research is situated at the point of impact, not in the qualification per se. Practice-based PhDs offer a means through which research activity can be de-institutionalised, the de-partitioning of academe from practice, and a challenge to the assumption that the production of new knowledge largely takes place in universities. In the post-truth era, institutions in general, from corporations to government and media, are distrusted to the extent that the challenge is political and not simply spatial, meaning architects will need to produce more than good design in order to demonstrate the value of their contribution to society. Whereas the spectre of the neoliberal university and the marketisation of higher education have placed an emphasis on the product rather than the process and the people,[11] architects in practice, given their closer

Fiona Zisch,
Allocentric View of Self,
Bartlett School of Architecture,
University College London (UCL),
2017–18

The photographs show a dancer navigating a labyrinth and learning a novel dance phrase with her choreographer while seeing herself from an allocentric (third-person) point of view in a virtual-reality headset.

proximity to the public, have an opportunity to reverse that trend and conduct research with civic and not just commercial impact.

By Whom, For Whom, With Whom?

One of the problems facing practice-based research is that architectural practice suffers from the same lack of diversity issues as higher education. If T-Levels (Technical-Level alternatives to A-Levels), the RIBA apprenticeships programme, Oxford Brookes University Office-Based Examination and the London School of Architecture's practice-based learning model all offer practical and more affordable routes to professional qualification, why should architecture practices with established R&D units not be permitted to gain licences to offer research degrees? For PhD candidates and even post-doctoral researchers, researching within a practice environment is likely to prove more immersive, relevant and affordable too. Making research the task of a paid worker rather than the price to pay for individual advantage and intellectual curiosity could further diversify architectural practice, and enable it to resist the representational disparities it inherited from architectural education, by obliterating tuition barriers. To widen research participation further, rather than treat the public as subjects or data sets, architects could adapt models of co-design into co-design research, and instead ethnographically empower the public in shaping research agendas and providing new ways of interpreting evidence based upon lived experience.

By giving architectural practice a future, architectural research ensures its own future, but it also gives practice the chance to imagine other futures where architecture's value, relevance and impact are no longer in any doubt

Kamil Dalkir,
Collective Equipment,
Objects / Bodies / Territories,
School of Architecture,
Royal College of Art (RCA),
London,
2016

above: The rocky terrain adjacent to the Korakas lighthouse and NGO shelter is littered with objects and clothing of the displaced arriving here from Turkish shores.

right: Once the residence of the island's Korakas lighthouse keeper, these disused and derelict buildings are utilised by the Lighthouse Relief NGO as medical facilities and shelter for those who are rescued.

Architecture, Automation and Inventive Autonomy

Even before the advent of the building information modelling (BIM) era, architects agonised over their ever-diminishing role within construction projects.[12] If the Bank of England predictions are correct and robots take over 15 million private-sector jobs within the next 10 years,[13] will Siri become a greater threat than subcontractors? Other analysts have identified that 85 per cent of jobs we will be doing in 2030 have yet to be invented,[14] calling into question not only the future of architectural research, but also the very existence of architectural practice. Yet is it correct to assume increased automation is necessarily a threat to architecture? Or could it facilitate more research activity by liberating architects from the many mundane and routine tasks required of contemporary architectural practice?

With robots designing the banal bits of buildings without employee overheads, practice income could resource the time needed for real academic freedom and experimentation, resulting in research processes and outcomes that fuel useful innovation and much-needed invention. Indeed, robots may even liberate institutionalised researchers from their funding-body-driven arranged marriages and redirect them towards better utilisation of their epistemologically agile three-dimensionally trained brains across an infinite number of professional contexts. Arguably, if architecture as both a discipline and a profession intends to count itself among the surviving 15 per cent of today's jobs still in existence in 2030, it is urgently obliged to identify new forms of practice and new applications for architectural knowledge and skills – and not to defend old notions of practice or obsolete ideological territories.

A Practice-Situated Future for Architectural Research?

Disciplines, much like building components or construction processes, become irrelevant if they are not put to use. As a consequence, architectural research is obligated to constantly assert its relevance in order to achieve meaningful impact. By situating architectural research in architectural practices, research is freed from the burden of expanding institutional overheads, disciplinary silos and academic ritualisation. It is also rendered more affordable, which serves to increase diversity of access and plurality of purpose. It can cultivate communities of enquiry with the people who inhabit them, sharing the benefits from research processes as well as outcomes. By reducing its physical proximity to persistent or emerging problems and opportunities, its ability to produce relevant outcomes is increased. As the era of automation approaches, all forms of research should work towards providing solutions to existing problems as often as they strive to discover new things. Architectural researchers who are by definition expert in working across a range of scales are especially equipped to address challenges as small as the structural collapse of a neuromorphic glial cell to one as large as the geospatial displacement of 27 million people caused by a structural collapse in political stability.[15] By giving architectural practice a future, architectural research ensures its own future, but it also gives practice the chance to imagine other futures where architecture's value, relevance and impact are no longer in any doubt. ⌁

Notes
1. See Andrew McGettigan, *The Great University Gamble: Money, Markets and the Future of Higher Education*, Pluto Press (London), 2013.
2. Sarah Stahlke Wall, 'Toward a Moderate Autoethnography', *International Journal of Qualitative Methods*, 15 (1), 2016, pp 1–9.
3. Brian Martin, 'The Politics of Research', *Information Liberation: Challenging the Corruptions of Information Power*, Freedom Press (London), 1998, pp 123–42.
4. Jennifer Rubin, UKRI to Tackle Diversity Problem in Research', *Times Higher Education*, 15 September 2018; https://www.timeshighereducation.com/blog/ukri-tackle-diversity-problem-research.
5. Higher Education Statistics Agency (HESA), 'Staff at Higher Education Providers in the United Kingdom 2015/16', 19 January 2017: www.hesa.ac.uk/news/19-01-2017/sfr243-staff, last accessed, 18/09/2018.
6. Jack Grove, 'One in Three UK Universities Going Backwards on Female Professorships', Times Higher Education, 25 May 2017; https://www.timeshighereducation.com/news/one-in-three-uk-universities-going-backwards-on-female-professorships.
7. The STM Report 2015, International Association of Scientific, Technical and Medical Publishers (The Hague), 2015; https://www.stm-assoc.org/2015_02_20_STM_Report_2015.pdf.
8. Laura Santhanam, 'Study Reveals Wide Gaps in Opinion Between Scientists and General Public', PBS NewsHour, 29 January 2015; www.pbs.org/newshour/science/study-reveals-wide-opinion-differences-scientists-general-public.
9. Andrew Abbott, *Chaos of Disciplines*, University of Chicago Press (Chicago, IL), 2010.
10. Bernard H Casey, 'The Economic Contribution of PhDs', *Journal of Higher Education Policy and Management*, 31 (3), 2009, pp 219–27.
11. Mike Molesworth, Richard. Scullion and Elizabeth Nixon, *The Marketisation of Higher Education and the Student as Consumer*, Routledge (Abingdon), 2010.
12. See Richard Waite, 'Over Two Thirds of Architects Want Exclusive Right to Design Buildings', *Architects' Journal*, 16 May 2014; www.architectsjournal.co.uk/news/over-two-thirds-of-architects-want-exclusive-right-to-design-buildings/8662620.article.
13. Cara McGoogan, 'Bank of England: 15 Million British Jobs at Risk from Robots', Wired, 13 November 2015; www.wired.co.uk/article/will-robots-take-your-job.
14. US Department of Labor, *Futurework: Trends and Challenges for Work in the 21st Century*, September 1999; www.dol.gov/oasam/programs/history/herman/reports/futurework/report.htm.
15. UNHCR, *Global Trends: Forced Displacement in 2017*, 19 June 2018; http://www.unhcr.org/uk/5b27be547.pdf#zoom=95.

Text © 2019 John Wiley & Sons Ltd. Images: pp 18–19, 24–5 © Kamil Dalkir; pp 21, 23 © Fiona Zisch

Public Planning Reimagined

Building Capacity and Agency

Frederik Weissenborn

Recent decades have seen knowledge-sharing across local-authority planning departments greatly diminished, with ever-dwindling numbers of architects employed in them. Countering these trends, non-profit social enterprise Public Practice places its associates in public bodies to champion innovation and embed research in the planning workflow. Its Research and Communications Manager **Frederik Weissenborn** describes how it functions.

Public Practice research topics workshop, London Metropolitan University, May 2018

Peer-to-peer learning is key to the R&D programme. During their placements, associates work closely together with each other and with the Public Practice team to define their research topics, and to learn about and troubleshoot complex planning-related issues.

The last 40 years have seen a drastic decline in the capacity and agency of local-authority planning departments in the UK. Not only have councils' powers to build homes been diminished, but the discipline of planning has splintered into multiple strands of expertise. As a consequence, knowledge that was previously shared centrally by planning departments now sits in isolated silos dispersed across council departments, consultants and agencies. Despite these challenging conditions, public planners continue to work hard to improve the built environment. However, the odds are stacked against them, with local authorities finding it increasingly difficult to attract new talent.

Public Practice is a not-for-profit social enterprise which is countering this trend by rebuilding public-sector capacity in the UK and developing new models of planning. Launched in 2017, it champions existing planners and attracts new practitioners to the profession through an innovative placement programme. Following years of outsourcing, the aim of the programme is to insource critical skills and knowhow into planning departments, and to help nurture a culture of excellence and innovation in public planning. This objective is achieved by placing built-environment professionals – known as 'associates' – within planning authorities and public bodies to build skills and cultivate expertise.

Cohort of associates,
Stratford,
London,
November 2018

Associates join local authorities and other public-sector organisations to boost planning capacity in the short term, and to help set up new processes to build capacity for the longer term.

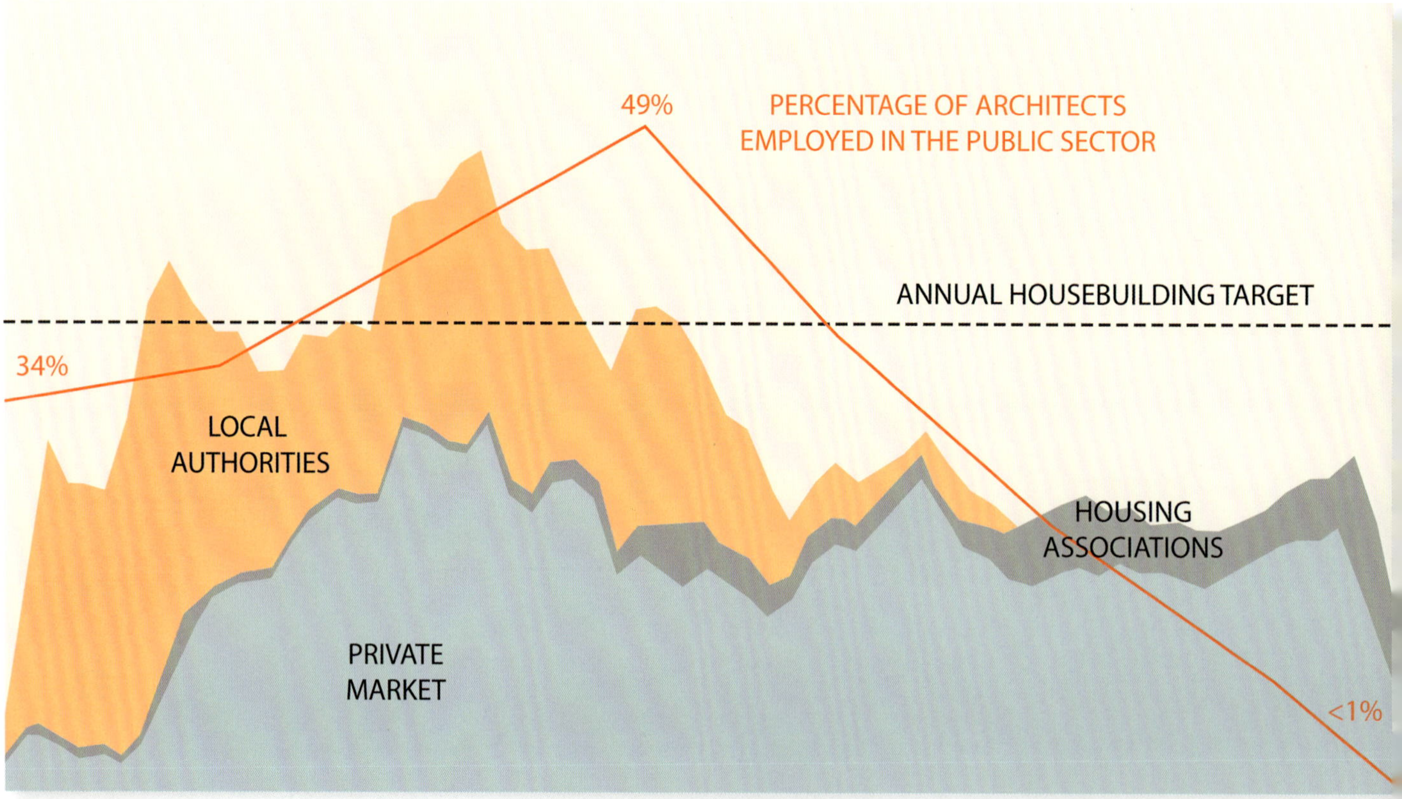

Public Practice,
Sector-by-sector overview of housing supply since the Second World War,
November 2018

As local-authority housing delivery has dwindled, so has the number of architects working in local government: now only 0.6 per cent of architects work in the public sector, compared to 49 per cent in the 1970s. Public Practice is part of a push to reverse this trend.

A Practice-Based Approach to Research and Development

Research and development plays a fundamental role in this process, with associates dedicating 10 per cent of their time to a collective R&D programme. At fortnightly R&D sessions, the cohort of associates is introduced to fundamental processes such as viability appraisals and models of public-sector procurement, and core skills such as strategies for negotiating S106 agreements (a mechanism that makes a development proposal acceptable in planning terms by mitigating the impact of the scheme). Public Practice also provides associates with user-centred design strategies to help them identify and explore opportunities for organisational innovation, and facilitate workshops on resilience to ensure that frontline experiences are shared and processed within the cohort.

The R&D programme also involves an associate-led research strand through which associates explore questions that authorities do not ordinarily have the capacity to address in order to develop new models of practice which are then shared across authority boundaries. This mix of activities, which includes technical knowledge, soft skills, personal development and horizon-scanning research, forms the basis of Public Practice's practice-based approach to research and development and is designed to promote and nurture institutional innovation in the public sector.

Public Practice,
R&D day,
Clerkenwell,
London,
June 2018

Together with invited experts, associates explore existing best practice – and develop new forms of 'next practice' – in planning and place-shaping.

Public Practice,
Reach of the first cohort of associates,
November 2018

Associates have been matched with roles in some of the most forward-thinking and ambitious local authorities and public bodies in the UK. Placements range from setting up council-led housebuilding programmes to shaping masterplans for new garden towns.

Public Practice associates
on a site visit,
Croydon,
April 2018

Associates meet for fortnightly R&D sessions, hosted at partnering local authorities, to develop new models of public planning and share emerging knowledge and practice. The structure varies and may include talks, debates, charrettes, masterclasses, panels, site visits and project reviews.

Leveraging a Community of Practice
Research projects are developed with the help of a wider community of practice to ensure relevance and implementability. Associates first scope research questions in collaboration with their host organisations in a process that encourages them to work with colleagues from different departments to collaboratively settle on the direction of their research. Public Practice then acts as a shared research department to filter and coordinate the questions, not only joining the dots across authorities, but also aligning research with a network of industry experts and academics.

Research projects are developed with the help of a wider community of practice to ensure relevance and implementability

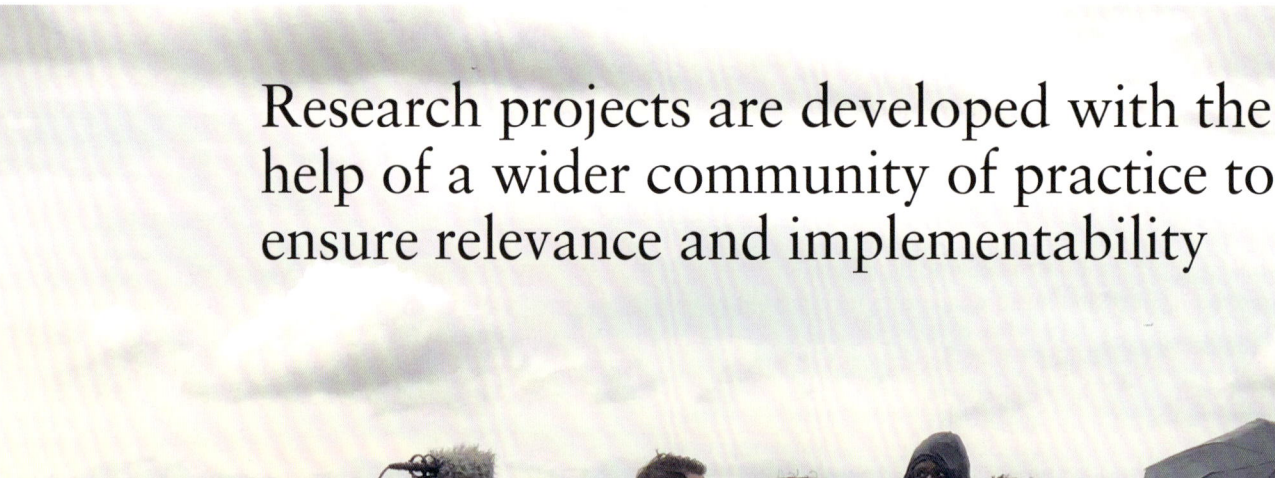

Following the initial scoping stage, research projects go through several iterations, during which associates gather insights to further define their understanding of the problem they are investigating and develop and test prototype solutions. The exact methodology varies from project to project and may include in-depth interviews, focus group discussions and surveys, but the research always involves active engagement with public planners and other experts in the field. The key is to learn from the people at the front line – the insights they have gathered as much as the challenges they face – and to operationalise that knowledge in practical research outcomes that can have a direct impact on public planning and provide it with new impetus and agency.

Learning from the Front Line

To take an example, in 2018 associates Ei-Lyn Chia and Sophie Palmer – placed respectively in the Greater London Authority (GLA) and the London Borough of Bexley – investigated new models for industrial intensification and co-location. During the scoping phase of their research, they organised workshops and panels with planners and the wider community of practice – including the policy teams working on the London Plan (the statutory spatial development strategy for the Greater London area), the GLA's Regeneration team, planners from Bexley, consultants, private developers and academics from the London Metropolitan University and Central Saint Martins – to develop a more nuanced understanding of the issue and explore ways of creatively reframing it.

Together with the Public Practice associate at the Old Oak and Park Royal Development Corporation (OPDC) – a mayoral corporation responsible for the development of a whole new centre and community in West London – they then organised a field trip to Brussels to explore models and solutions trialled there, and to gain an international perspective. In addition to site visits, the field trip included a series of intensive workshops with representatives from the city's public planning agencies, during which insights were gathered, findings discussed and potential solutions explored.

The evidence gathered during the field trip and the preceding scoping phase enabled the associates to further refine the framework for their research into industrial intensification. They then explored how a combination of factors – including a lack of economic incentives for co-location, inadequate planning mechanisms, and lack of methods to reach out to local businesses – had contributed to the current state of affairs, and sought ways of reframing and unlocking the problem. Findings from their research were presented as a report in April 2019.

Broadening Agency

The framework that associates develop their research through is loose and process-oriented, but embodies a deliberate design. The iterative and collaborative approach ensures they can move fast with their research and quickly begin to develop and test workable solutions. Research outputs include tools, templates and tactics that are useful for officers to implement; for example, new kinds of legal clauses to secure design quality, hacks to integrate new digital technologies within councils' IT systems, or guidance for an alternative approach to public procurement. These outputs are disseminated to authorities and organisations in Public Practice's network and made public on its website. Over time, the research produced through this programme will help build a shared design culture within local authorities that can contribute to the promotion of strategic thinking and broaden the agency of public planning. ⌁

Text © 2019 John Wiley & Sons Ltd. Images: pp 26–7, 28(b), 29-31 © Public Practice; p 28(t) ©Tim Smyth

Practise What You Preach

Lara Kinneir

The University as a Common Ground Between Research and its Application

Is the mainstream university system really the right place to nurture the architects of tomorrow? It was this question that prompted the foundation in 2015 of the London School of Architecture. Not only does the school link education to the profession through student engagement with London's urban stakeholders and decision-makers; it also makes architectural education affordable by incorporating time in paid employment into the programme. **Lara Kinneir**, who leads its compulsory Urban Studies module, explains how it all works.

> Everyone wants to design.
> Doesn't anyone want to think?
> —Urban-Think Tank, 2006[1]

London School of Architecture (LSA),
The City is Our Campus,
London,
2017

Students study in the city, connecting with daily life. Each two-year cohort focuses its studies in one London borough, enabling thorough investigation and networking with local stakeholders.

If a research paper is published, and its hypothesis proven, but no one acts on it, should the paper even exist? The World Bank found that more than 31 per cent of its policy reports are never downloaded and 87 per cent never cited. Around 49 per cent of its reports have the stated objective of informing public debate or influencing community development. It invests $93 million annually in achieving this objective and publishing these unread reports.[2]

Each year hundreds of built-environment research projects are commissioned across London by private, public, academic and civic sectors. Though they attempt to address critical issues, their afterlife is at best a second thought, and often not considered until the research is complete. This results in missed opportunities to act upon the findings of these documents, which lie lost and ignored on dust-ridden shelves or on neglected hard drives.

The London School of Architecture (LSA) is interested in design as a process as well as an output. Fundamental to this design process is the production of knowledge and its application for the betterment of the built environment. Its academic programme strives to educate students in the crucial dialogue between knowledge and its application through a continual process of critical reflection from within and outside of the school. In doing so, a new common ground is created, fuelled by research and practice, providing a petri dish for the students' studies throughout the two-year programme.

A New Route

The school originated when its founder Will Hunter, then the deputy editor of the *Architectural Review*, published an article in 2012 proposing 'Alternative Routes For Architecture' (ARFA) in order to challenge conventional models for architectural education and asking professionals and academics for their thoughts. As Hunter questioned: 'Are architecture schools housed within the state-controlled university system really the best place to create the next generation of architects?[3]

The response to the article and subsequent years of discussion and planning led to its inauguration only three years later in 2015 with a 30-strong group of students. It now has 60 alumni and 80 current students, with application numbers doubling each year as the thirst for a new route for architectural education and practice increases.

At the outset, the school had three main objectives. Firstly, to build a link between education, practice and the profession at a fundamental level. Secondly, to reshape the relationship between academia and the research that happens within London's architectural and other built-environment practices, focusing students intensively on real design issues in the capital. By engaging with the stakeholders that shape the city, the student cohorts create proposals that can have real impact, guided by a teaching group of practising architects – the Practice Network. And thirdly, to provide a cost-effective way for students to study architecture. In the current model, first-year students are employed and paid in practice three days each week, with the remaining time spent in school. This effectively provides a cost-neutral way for students to further their architectural education alongside making the critical link between what they are learning and how they can implement it.

Impact Learning

The LSA's manifesto identifies five prime values: propositional, relevant, innovative, metropolitan and entrepreneurial. Embedded within its teaching model is the conviction that there is a dynamic and critical conversation to be had between students, teachers and practitioners and the context within which they are practising and for whom. This is facilitated in multiple different ways, involving many participants in varying situations, to create a continual two-way dialogue. The LSA students debate with stakeholders, engage with decision makers, pitch new approaches to funders, and self-initiate projects they have identified as opportunities for improving the city. Through this, a common platform for the student-practitioner is formed to enable new knowledge that has operational significance for their practice. Adopting what Linda Candy defines as a 'practice-led' rather than a 'practice-based' approach, the intention is to generate data about the professional context via the research modality conventionally referred to as 'reflections on practice'.[4]

London School of Architecture (LSA),
Design Think Tank meeting at Second Home,
London,
2015

Students discuss their research with their Practice Leaders, practitioners who dedicate time to collaborating with them on research topics. They meet in spaces around the city, which allows them to experience other working environments and connect with professionals from a variety of backgrounds.

London School of Architecture (LSA),
Urban Studies – The New Old Kent Road,
London,
2017

Following an in-depth study of the proposed regeneration for this area of Southeast London, students mediated the challenges and opportunities of old and new to create a vision for current and future users.

The City is Our Campus

The school's studies focus on London, the city in which it is based. This enables students to apply their research as investigations are carried out, and offers a 'practice-led' approach to the context. This continually growing body of knowledge of London is considered within other urban contexts as part of the LSA's commitment to investigating the application of the UN Sustainable Development Goals, which creates connections to a global family of researchers.

Uniquely, the programme begins with Urban Studies, which unlike at most other schools is a compulsory module. This was a very deliberate decision: the city is our campus, and we must therefore understand it to be able to offer the most successful opportunities for change. The design of cities, and the social, economic and political processes that contribute to the making and remaking of urban environments, specifically within the context of London, is what drives the agenda. Each two-year cohort studies a specific London borough, enabling them to gain a breadth and depth of understanding for a particular part of the city, and to identify a specific line of inquiry that often carries them through to their final thesis.

Within the exercises they are set, students are given the opportunity to play a central role in how the collaborative design decisions that shape the urban future are made. As a result, they are equipped to be the agents of change the city is currently lacking.

Another very deliberate positioning is that the most research-focused moment occurs during the first year of the programme. In the Design Think Tank module, Practice Network practitioners and students work in direct alignment on a 14-week research project, the aim of which is to produce a new form of architectural output.

The key outcomes of the Design Think Tanks have revealed tangible benefits in connecting research with practice. As Rae Whittow-Williams, Senior Project Officer at the Greater London Authority (GLA) says: 'Through my involvement as co-leader of a Design Think Tank, we have got the students to consider their proposals in line with various Mayoral strategies, including how they fit in with the recently launched Draft New London Plan and the London Infrastructure Plan 2050. We've used our GLA Group contacts to get the students to present to professionals involved in their area of study, which has enabled "real world" feedback, and a testing of their project in a professional environment. In this sense, I think we can really see the benefits of connecting research with practice; the resulting schemes are so much richer in terms of their contextual awareness to the issues we are facing within the built environment sector'.[5]

Working in an architectural office alongside their studies allows students to gain a view from the ground. As part of the Critical Practice modules that parallel the Urban Studies and Design Think Tanks components, they are asked to develop a 'Critical Practice Manual', a detailed research tool that is an ongoing project conducted over a period of eight months. Using the workplace as the principal site of investigation, the manual explores the relationship between process and product, ideas and outcomes. Through this, a dynamic relationship is formed that oscillates between participating in the day-to-day running of an architectural practice and standing back in order to interrogate it. Further fuelling the growth of the school's role as a common ground between research and application, the practice networks are invited to engage in the process to leverage the opportunity to develop their own ideas as well as those of the students.

Studio Culture

A continual thread throughout all modules is the design studio, where all research from inside and outside of the school is brought to the table and discussed. Design is the school's currency and is therefore at the core of the common platform it seeks to provide, where students' projects can exist within both the school studio and their practice placement, and where they can use the different contexts to feed off one another, to learn, adjust and nudge.

This shared platform has created a learning experience that rewards both students and practitioners, who have reported that the student research has in turn informed, enlightened and adapted their own forms of practice. The collaborative nature of participating in a common platform as well as the particular approach to research the school instils throughout its programme ensures it is just as much about what is taught as how it is taught, and ultimately how students can become the agents of change our cities need.

London School of Architecture (LSA), Urban Studies – Design Reviews, London, 2017

During a two-way conversation, students receive commentary on their work from guest design critics chosen from a wide network for their expertise and relevance to the students' lines of inquiry.

A dynamic relationship is formed that oscillates between participating in the day-to-day running of an architectural practice and standing back in order to interrogate it

Robin Chatwin,
Public Luxury,
London School of
Architecture (LSA),
2018

As our local authorities struggle to afford basic services, this student proposal takes existing buildings owned by the council and upgrades and extends them so that they contain and offer more public services.

Outputs and Opportunities

After two complete cycles, a wide range of module outputs and design thesis projects continue to be tested in the city beyond the end of the module or two-year programme. With rigour and ingenuity, the students have addressed critical issues such as civic services, housing shortages, infrastructure growth and social cohesion alongside less familiar challenges such as urban burial sites, food waste and mental health in an urban context. An example is one student's investigation of local authorities' struggle to afford basic services. The resulting proposal, entitled Public Luxury, upgrades and extends existing council-owned buildings to expand the social and urban potential of what are already public spaces to the point where they are able to do and provide things no other body can. The work has proved to be a timely and influential thesis in the current debate and decision-making processes surrounding the future of local authorities and their property portfolios.

Another project, Wasteminster, demonstrated a new model for small-scale infrastructure that tackles London's urban food waste and led to the student joining forces with a fellow LSA student to form a practice upon graduation to continue this work. Their research was reported in a three-part series in London's Evening Standard in 2018 and continues to gain momentum.

As part of the Design Think Tank module, a group of students set out to explore architecture's potential in the sharing economy, searching for a new mode of practice to connect people, places and practitioners in the hope of creating vibrant and diverse cities. Their proposal, SWARM, is a digitally connected and ever-evolving network of individuals that links those with expertise to those with a desire to transform the city. The school's alumni continue to debate, develop and present the concept to potential funders and supporters.

A Future of Design

Within the context of the city, we do not have to look far to realise that the process of design is something that is sorely missing outside of the design studio. LSA students are set the mission of bringing design out of its comfort zone and into the heart of places that currently lack a cycle of observation, proposition, speculation and reflection. This spatial intelligence is a rare but critical skill that must be used to impact change, with an education system that supports this.

As one of its major predictions for the built environment for 2020, global trend company WGSN has listed the emergence of 'urban observers'.[6] This is something architects have been doing for quite a while, but perhaps we have forgotten how to communicate our core skills in observing and creating routes of application.

Evening Standard,
London,
2018

LSA student research on waste in the city led to a series of articles in London's daily newspaper on the wider impact of this global challenge.

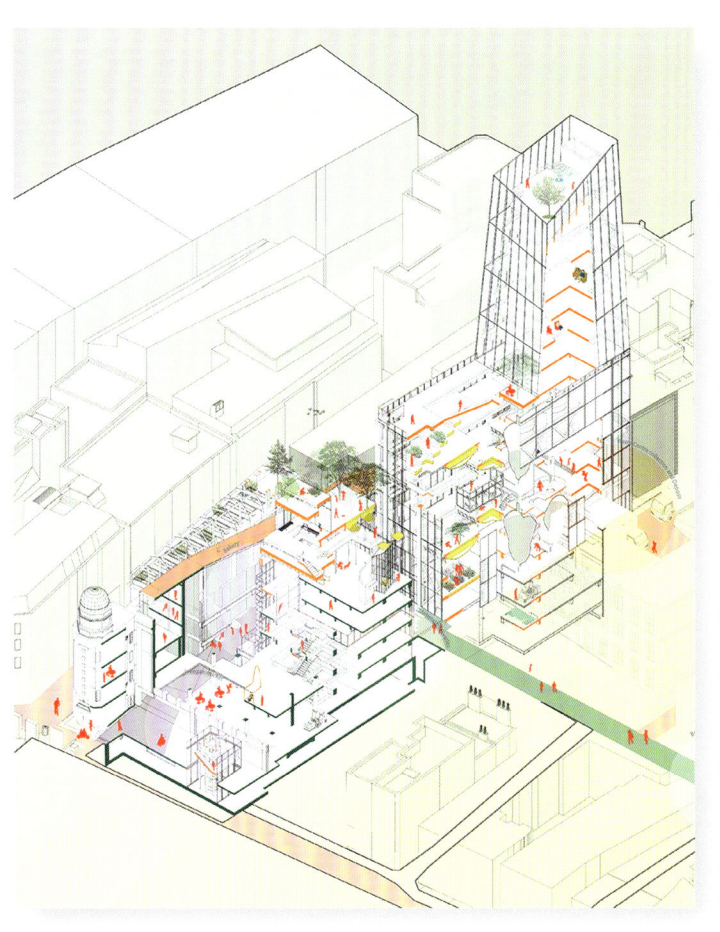

As the school continues to grow, so too will its portfolio of programmes. It will continue to reflect and connect with other education models trailblazing the need for a new relationship between research and practice. One such model is the Stanford University Human Cities Initiative in California, which nurtures an interdisciplinary community of faculty, students and community stakeholders. Another is the Gauteng City-Region Observatory (GCRO) in Johannesburg, which was established (and funded) by the provincial government in partnership with two of the city's universities to, among other things, enable a more functionally integrated and spatially coherent region.

In the LSA's quest to further the common ground between practice and profession, and to reshape the relationship between academia and research by focusing students intensively on relevant design issues within London, it will strive to continue to support and showcase student design theses that offer real, innovative and entrepreneurial proposals that can change the city for the better. Its alumni are already leading this change through their early career trajectories, which include setting up their own practices upon graduation, joining government design teams and receiving design commissions from developers and local authorities based on their work within the school's two-year programme. Their outputs do not stay on the shelf or in dusty drawers, because the LSA has created a dialogue that is informing practice. The future for these students is bright, and as a result, the school's is too. ᴅ

Aleks Stovjakovic,
Wasteminster,
London School of Architecture (LSA),
2016

Food waste costs the average person in London £200 a year, rising to £700 for a family with children. Wasteminster addresses this by providing holistic economic incentives, new forms of innovative construction, food-growing operations, a recycling institute, materials-testing labs and a hotel that promotes communal living and sustainable cycles in the heart of London's Soho.

Notes
1. Urban-Think Tank, Caracas Think Tank, 2006.
2. Doerte Doemeland and James Trevino, 'Which World Bank Reports Are Widely Read?', World Bank Policy Research Working Paper 6851, 1 May 2014; http://documents.worldbank.org/curated/en/387501468322733597/Which-World-Bank-reports-are-widely-read.
3. Will Hunter, 'Alternative Routes for Architecture', *Architectural Review*, 28 September 2012;
www.architectural-review.com/today/alternative-routes-for-architecture/8636207.article.
4. Linda Candy, 'Practice Based Research: A Guide', Creativity & Cognition Studios (Sydney), 2006; www.creativityandcognition.com/resources/PBR%20Guide-1.1-2006.pdf.
5. Rae Whittow-Williams, LSA module feedback, London, 2018.
6. WGSN, 'Key Macro Trends', *The Vision 2020*, 2018.

LSA Summer Exhibition,
London,
2017

Students present work and curate a series of events that allow them to develop opportunities to implement their proposals through debates and meeting with key stakeholders, funders and the design professions.

Text © 2019 John Wiley & Sons Ltd. Images: pp 33, 34(t), 36(t), 37 Courtesy of LSA; pp 34(b), 36(b) Courtesy Lara Kinneir; p 35 © LSA

Leon van Schaik

How did the artificial division arise between research and practice in architecture, why is it a problem, and how can it be reversed? The RMIT University School of Architecture and Urban Design in Melbourne, Australia has been pioneering practice-embedded research for three decades, with a PhD programme that has inspired similar approaches at other institutions across the world. Having identified five continuums between research and practice that are required to maximise the potential of architecture, Emeritus Professor **Leon van Schaik**, who initiated the programme, explores its impact through the work of some of its participants.

NING NUUMS

Leon van Schaik, Continuums ideogram, 2018

opposite: The ideogram relates the design of the Highgate School in Perth, Western Australia by iredale pedersen hook architects to the concepts in the author's book *Architecture in its Continuum*s (Uro, Melbourne, 2018).

Addressing the Separation of Research and Practice in Architecture

Having failed to claim its own unique knowledge base, the profession of architecture has developed a dysfunctional relationship with its academies and with adjacent professions. This lapse has also rent the continuum between everyday life experience and architectural practice. Where in sport everyone who plays ball games has some ownership of elite performance, in architecture the confusion about the knowledge that the profession nurtures on behalf of society renders esoteric the benefits of great design. What is the unique knowledge base? It is spatial thinking based on our spatial intelligence.[1] I contend that to make successful designs and maximise the benefits for our discipline, we must consider the five continuums of architecture – knowing and being; expertise; scholarship; practice; and ethics – which rely on a strong connection between research and practice.[2] These continuums can currently only be integrated with practice through research.

How Were the Continuums Broken?

As architecture ceased to be an apprenticeship enlivened by lectures by practitioners such as John Soane (1753–1837 – at the Royal Academy, in his case), and it entered the university system, an artificial division between practice and research was created even though universities did not feel the need to enforce the same separation in medicine, law or other practice-based professions. Further, in its struggle to find its own niche, architecture has cut itself off from decorating, interior deign and landscape architecture, breaching a profound continuum. Engineering, by contrast, has a professional structure that nests all the different levels of expertise in a framework of mutual esteem. The result of broken continuums has been the creation in architecture schools of an esoteric body of theory that is not interpreted or informed by practitioners, and has therefore no role in the furthering of good practice. It is as if medical practitioners had only alchemy to guide them. The separation, embraced by academics, has resulted in research about the history, sociology and environmental science of architecture, rather than research grounded in the mediums of practice, and this has been deleterious to both practice and the education of architects.

The constants of architecture are reasonably well served in the academies. For example, Steen Eiler Rasmussen (1898–1990) expanded on the qualities of light, form and materiality – identifying solids and cavities composed of matter that is carved or moulded; surfaced to look hard, soft or translucent; textured or decorated; raw or with applied colour; penetrated with openings or articulated with markings that are rhythmically and proportionally arrayed; and with sound and scent brought into play.[3] In the digital era these constants are joined by pixilation and the amplification or suppression of data. However, typically there is a lack of concern for the continuums in the academies, and practice grapples with the continuums without the support of the schools. Unless students are made aware of their own histories in space – the spatial preferences that colour their designs – they become practitioners who unwittingly export their prejudices to the communities that they serve, rather than engaging in a conscious dialogue about the spatial expectations of people who more often than not have histories in space that are not shared by the designer.

The architecture programme at Melbourne's RMIT University has aimed to mend this tear by developing over three decades a scholarship of practice-embedded research that seeks to surface the tacit knowledge that underpins great designing. The knowledge gained has been used to structure the studio culture of the school. More recently the London School of Architecture (LSA) has gone even further in its determination to bridge the chasm, embedding its students in the research streams in a network of over 100 London practices. This venture is very much the brainchild of the LSA's director Will Hunter, and while it probably benefits from the current state of the British economy, it is driven by Will's vision. He edited the October 2012 issue of *Architectural Review* on the theme of what is wrong with architectural education, and its follow-up in October 2013 on what is right in architectural education. The former identified the chasm between practice and the academies, the latter identified RMIT as a rare example of scholarship that integrated practice and research.

There were no exceptional factors in the Australian environment that enabled the emergence of the design practice research programme at RMIT. As a practitioner-academic entering an academic leadership role, primed by knowledge of similar programmes in other professions and inspired by the exceptional but unsung work of practitioners in Melbourne, I set about inviting architects who were held in high regard by their peers, with a significant body of work extending over a period of several years, to enter a critical framework to examine the nature of the mastery that they had established. (The ideogram illustrated provides an example of the critical frame at work.) This is essentially how the programme continues to operate – in Melbourne, in Barcelona and other European cities, and in Ho Chi Minh City and other Asian cities. One factor supporting the model is that doctoral completions in a research programme that has manifest benefits to the industry that it serves attract funding to the host institution.

Benefits to Practitioners

Practitioners who have participated in the research programme at RMIT report that they have become more able to describe to potential clients what their design process is, how the client will be involved, and how the outcome will be forged. They find that it has made them more conscious of the ways in which they work, and about giving those ways an expressed form in their practices. Many have found the research has led to far more fulsome engagements with client bodies and user clients. Certainly in Melbourne and the

Stuart Geddes,
Cover artwork of *By Practice, By Invitation: Design Practice Research in Architecture and Design at RMIT, 1986–2011*

The volume, which has become known as 'the Pink Book', celebrated the 25th anniversary of the RMIT research programme.

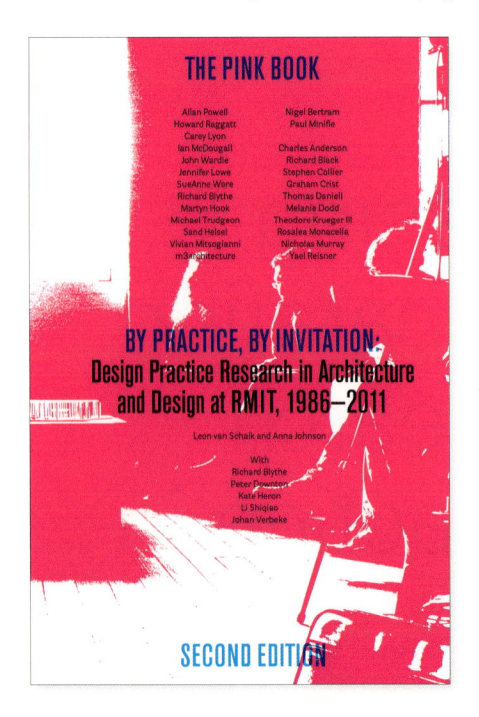

other major cities where the programme has had an influence, architects who have been through the programme win a large share of commissions and awards.⁴ Some developers have taken advantage of this. The redevelopment of a city block in central Melbourne became known as the 'RMIT alumni project', so many of the buildings were designed by recent graduates of the programme. Observing this, a major commercial practice asked me to run a programme in-house for their designers. While this did not eventuate in Melbourne, the research approach has been used in compressed form to assist groups that have gingered up the design efforts of large international practices such as AECOM and ONG&ONG in Singapore. In the latter case, so successful did the group become at winning competitions, that we were lobbied to discontinue the short course.

What Does Research Through Design Practice Look Like?

The practitioners who are involved in the programme reflect on and describe the mental space that has been developed as their platform for change, their practical poetics of designing. Scores of practices have accepted the invitation, amongst these Deborah Saunt of DSDHA. Following an exhaustive analysis of her practice's work, Deborah discovered that the most successful projects were conducted within a carefully structured office conversation that engaged, at varying levels, all of the intelligences available.⁵ This led to a more curated approach to the creation of such conversations around projects. Tom Holbrook of 5th Studio, another participant in the research programme, who focused on the ways in which his firm conjured projects out of little more than a strategic interest in regional development processes, also refined his practice's conversational processes.

Insights Emerging from Recent Research

In the course of monitoring the practitioners in this research programme, supervisors become aware of a treasure trove of evidence about design practice. What follows is a selection of these, grouped according to the practice nature.⁶

A first category comprised small practices run by practitioner academics. Among these were Alice Casey and Cian Deegan of TAKA in Dublin, who completed their research in 2017. Alice researched the modes of design in her practice, revealing especially how details are developed in a conversation between the design idea, what other architects have built and a contractor's capabilities. She discovered that the geometry of the seemingly simple wall capping defied resolution, and even the advice of her most experienced peers and mentors did not help until inducted into a full conversation with her partner and the builder. She realised that she was mostly interested in the pragmatics of the practice. Cian on the other hand concentrated on the ways in which the desired decorum of their work was enlivened

Alice Casey,
Stepped beam for Merrion Cricket Pavilion,
Dublin,
from PhD dissertation,
RMIT School of Architecture and Urban Design,
Melbourne,
2017

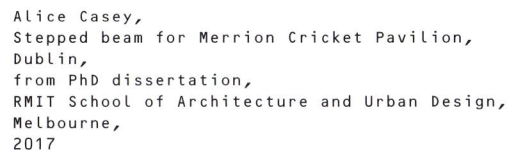

Casey – co-founder of TAKA Architects, Dublin – uncovered the multi-layered conversations with mentors, peers and the contractor as the realisation of this deceptively simple detail of a stepped beam was resolved.

Siobhán Ní Éanaigh,
Field,
from PhD dissertation,
RMIT School of Architecture
and Urban Design, Melbourne,
2018

The painting was produced during Siobhán Ní Éanaigh's research into the role of colour in her practice.

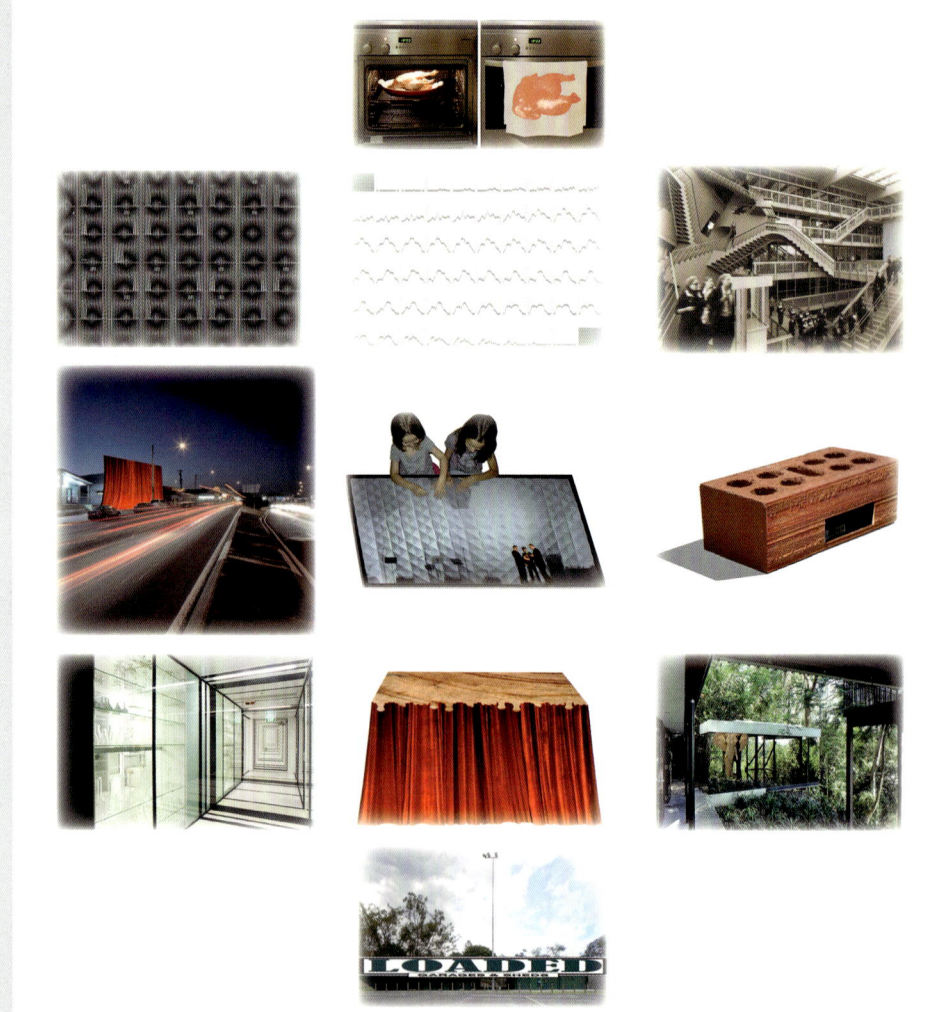

Michael Banney,
*Inventory of 'old habits' –
anecdotal evidence*,
from PhD dissertation,
RMIT School of Architecture
and Urban Design, Melbourne,
2017

In this image, Banney, founding director of Brisbane firm m3architecture, records the research platform from which he launched his investigation into the use of anecdotes in his designing.

specificity that surprises
anecdote

Siobhán Ní Éanaigh / McGarry Ní Éanaigh Architects,
Coláiste Ailigh School,
County Donegal,
Ireland,
2013

The internal corridor shows the use of super-saturated colour characteristic of the practice's designs. The colour intensity continues externally: deep blue in this case, crimson and scarlet in another.

by the ways in which they sought out exotic exemplars on journeys that targeted experience beyond their own civil and urbane location.

In the same category, another Dublin-based duo, Andrew Clancy and Colm Moore, who also completed in 2017, tracked in their design process their own conversations and those with the makers of their projects. Using videos of their tabletop drawing sessions, and distillations of the key moments in text and in drawings, they realised that for them, a project is not a design until it expresses the tensions inherent in resolving brief, site and regulatory constraints in a 'figure', and that their projects are choreographies of 'figures'. This insight supported the design work current in their studio.

Secondly, there were niche practices. Of these, Anthony Hoete, who completed in 2016, examined his practice, WHAT architecture (London), and came to see it as a 'Game of Architecture' governed by rules and constraints. Concentrating on a 'Game of Housing', he proposes an operating fieldwork of rules and roles to enable and empower his practice to continue to be a 'game-changer'. Completing the following year was Robert Simeoni, an award-winning Melbourne architect who explored the ways a systematic process of observing and capturing moments of informal architectural invention in his neighbourhood, and in the North Italy of his origins, informs his design practice.

A third category consisted of practices with a significant national presence in their countries. In researching his design methodology, Michael Banney of the much-awarded Brisbane office m3architecture, who completed in 2017, discovered three ways in which he creates and uses anecdotes while developing design strategies. Stories are retrieved from his archive of memories or spontaneously engendered in real time from stimuli in the environment of projects. He found it liberating to discover that he works in this way. Siobhán Ní Éanaigh of McGarry Ní Éanaigh Architects, Dublin, completed in 2018. Researching her joint practice – one that has transformed the designing of schools in Ireland – she examined the ways in which she suffuses designs with a spaciousness inflected by strategically chosen saturated colour.

MvS Architects,
RMIT New Academic Street,
Melbourne,
2018

View of new inter-level access from Swanston
Street, the civic spine of Melbourne.

The Conversations Through Which Architecture is 'Made Up'
In most cases, as with the research conducted by Deborah Saunt, the findings involve the ways in which architects bring their own mental spaces into play in a richly inclusive design environment, illuminated by their own particular ways of, as Peter Cody puts it, 'making architecture up'.[7] Illustrated here is Jan van Schaik's diagram of the mental space from which he 'fakes it till he makes it'. 'Bruegelage' was the expressive title that he gave to the dissertation arising from his research.[8] The word conveys how teeming intelligences are brought together to create outcomes that surprise and delight clients, create work opportunities and produce learning environments. The illustrated design from his practice's recently completed New Academic Street at RMIT conveys some of the qualities that have imbued subsequent work.

More often than not, the research commences with establishing what the practice does, and how extensive the span of its work is. Inventories of works completed are made, and they often surprise, as this is usually the first time reflection has taken place. When iredale pedersen hook architects began their research, they confidently stated that they had completed one hundred and fifty projects. When the alley outside their office in Perth, Western Australia closed they lined it with trestle tables and brought out the models that had accumulated over a decade of practice. By the evening we counted three hundred projects! And already they were putting like with like and getting a grasp of the themes that run through their designing in a new way while gaining fresh insights.

Through this type of research, Robert Simeoni 'nailed' the mental spaces in which he designs and finds himself in command of the deep structures of his intuition, able to call upon it at will. Allan Powell feared initially that investigating 'the magic' of his sensibility would dissipate it. Instead he came to regard his intuition as a sturdy horse, available at any time to carry him across difficulties in a design. Siobhán Ní Éanaigh now understands how she selects and applies colour. Consciousness is at the core here, the researchers understand how their intelligences work, and are able to describe to potential clients precisely what they offer, and in terms that go way beyond the standard public-relations mantras of 'on time, to budget'. And those of us who design learning environments have real knowledge on which to base what we do.

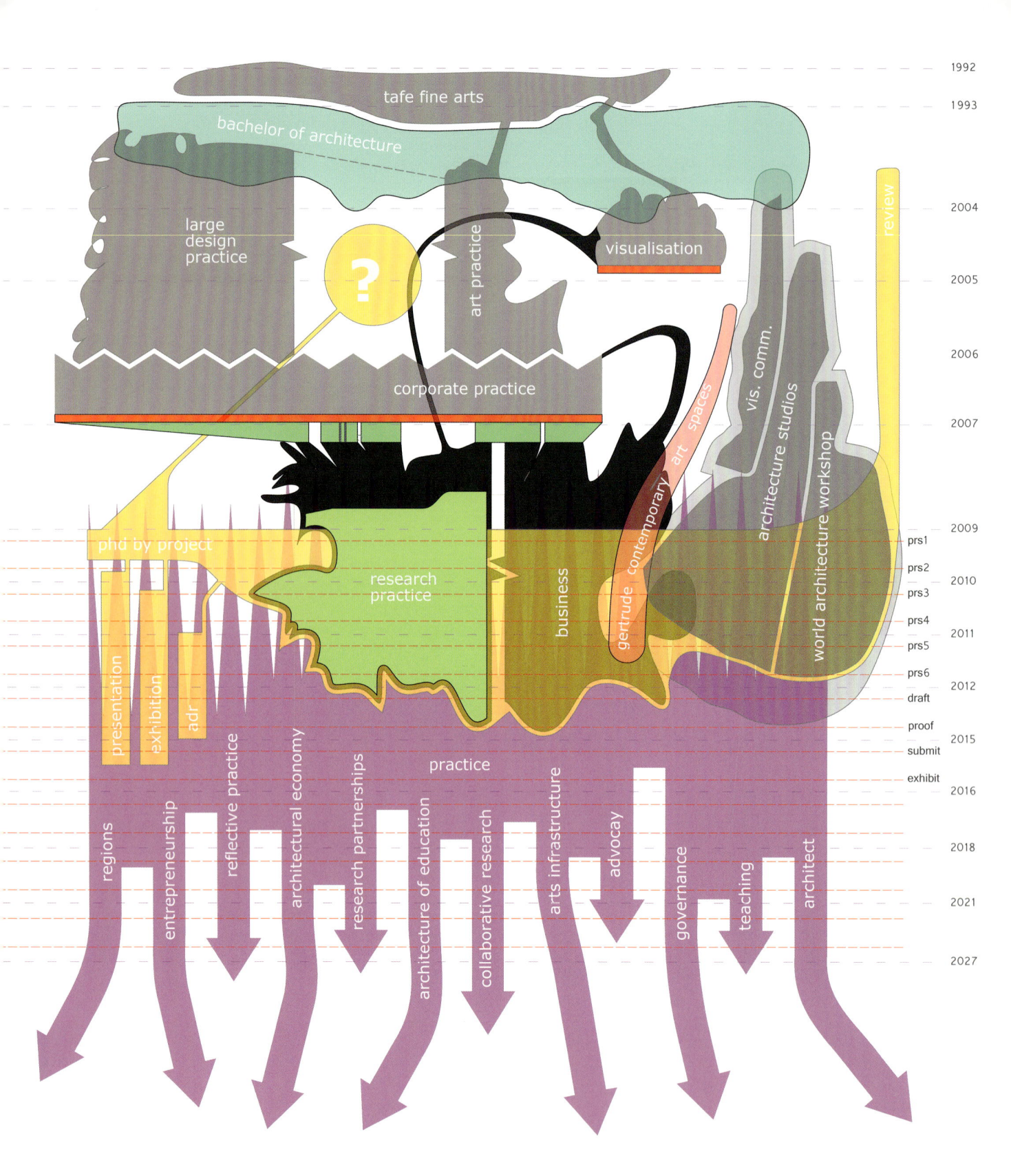

Jan van Schaik,
Research diagram showing practice and process of reflection,
from PhD dissertation,
RMIT School of Architecture and Urban Design, Melbourne,
2017

Featured in his dissertation titled 'Breugelage: Interrogations into Nine Concurrent Creative Practices', the diagram by Jan van Schaik, co-founder of MvS Architects, illustrates the architect's mental space during the design process.

The Continuums Restored at RMIT

As a university RMIT demonstrates to students that it acts as it teaches. As a commissioning client RMIT has adopted the research by structuring its processes of appointment around detailed assessments of how consultants, shortlisted (in ranges depending on the complexity of the project at hand) for their design ambition, lateral and sustainable thinking capacities, approach the business of meeting and developing the client brief.[9]

The most important gap in education lies in its failure to accept that the core knowledge base of architecture (landscape architecture, urban design, interior design, decoration) lies in spatial thinking developed from the spatial intelligence with which all of us are endowed. No other professional cluster has the capability to address problems spatially. Practitioners who engage in our research programme become conscious of the mental space that they create in order to design, and in so doing become more enabled in accessing their deep knowledge, their intuition. Making students aware of this process is one way in which RMIT addresses the gap. Another is in ensuring that students all have the opportunity to have studio experiences hosted by practices that have been through the research programme. But most importantly, we educators need to add to the inculcation into the texts and designs of the various canons of our disciplines, a process by which students become aware of their histories in space, the ways in which their spatial thinking has been formed. This is rather like making fish aware of water. Until people are removed from their normative spatial environments, they do not know that they have such a thing! ∆

Robert Simeoni,
Inventory,
from PhD dissertation,
RMIT School of Architecture and Urban Design,
Melbourne,
2017

Simeoni made two major inventories in his research. One captured the buildings of North Melbourne that framed his spatial history. The other, sampled here, documented objects, books and images that frame his mental space.

Notes
1. See Leon van Schaik, *Spatial Intelligence: New Futures for Architecture*, John Wiley & Sons (Chichester), 2008.
2. See Leon van Schaik, *Architecture in its Continuums*, Uro (Melbourne), 2018.
3. See Steen Eiler Rasmussen, *Experiencing Architecture*, Chapman and Hall (London), 1964.
4. Leon van Schaik, *Design City Melbourne*, Wiley-Academy (Chichester), 2006 documents the phenomenon in the city.
5. Leon van Schaik, *Practical Poetics in Architecture*, John Wiley & Sons (Chichester), 2015, pp 164–71.
6. These researches as dissertations and as filmed presentations are all accessible through https://researchbank.rmit.edu.au/adv_search.php and provide a rich resource for anyone engaged in the business of research.
7. Peter Cody, 'Practical Fiction', PhD dissertation, RMIT School of Architecture and Urban Design, 2017, p 90: https://researchbank.rmit.edu.au/view/rmit:162321.
8. Jan van Schaik, 'Breugelage: Interrogations into Nine Concurrent Creative Practices', PhD dissertation, RMIT School of Architecture and Urban Design, 2016: https://researchbank.rmit.edu.au/view/rmit:161567.
9. See Leon van Schaik and Geoffrey London, *Procuring Innovative Architecture*, Routledge (London), 2010, pp 14–28, 29–31.

Text © 2019 John Wiley & Sons Ltd. Images: p 38 © Leon van Schaik; p 40 © Stuart Geddes; p 41 ©TAKA Architects/Alice Clancy (photo); pp 42(t), 43 © Siobhan Ni Einaigh; p 42(b) © Michael Banney; pp 44-5 © Peter Bennetts; p 46 © Drawing by Jan van Schaik, 2015; p 47 © Robert Simeoni

James Soane

Project Orange,
Zone Hotels,
India,
2014

The studio's early collage study for the design of the four-star Zone Hotels chain in India, as featured in Emma Elston's 'Rules and Representation' essay in *PO Box 2*. The concept seeks to establish a connection between traveller and place by creating a contemporary collage of the country and its traditions.

Out of Practice

Theoretical Speculations In and Out of the Business of Architecture

Sharing reflections on their practice is a core part of how members of London-based architecture and interior design studio Project Orange operate. One of the studio's co-founders, **James Soane**, describes how they came to publish a series of zines, each edited by a different prestigious academic, that have not only nurtured the research-led nature of their work but also fed into the teaching approach at the London School of Architecture.

Judgement of architecture is deferred to the market. The 'architectural style' of buildings no longer conveys an ideological choice but a commercial one.[1]
—Reinier de Graaf, 'Architecture is Now a Tool of Capital', 2015

What is practice-based research, and how does it relate to the business of architecture? This is a question that interests research-led architecture and interior design studio Project Orange. While it is commonly understood that architects undertake research in the form of learning about new technologies or discovering the latest specification, this is generally under the umbrella of continuing professional development (CPD). As the Royal Institute of British Architects (RIBA) notes, CPD is required for all chartered architects to stay competent, professional, capable and resilient. Members are expected to engage in 35 hours per year that are logged. Amongst its 10 core topics are: architecture for social purpose; health, safety and wellbeing; business, clients and services; legal, regulatory and statutory compliance; and design, construction and technology.[2]

The perception that the profession is only interested in technical know-how supports a situation where the CPD curriculum excludes new kinds of knowledge and critical reflection: the wider societal impact of architecture, how and why design matters and the values it embodies. It is therefore imperative that architects develop research strands to challenge this narrow compliance culture and to test their intuition.

Research Through Reflection

The distance between academia, as symbolised by the rarefied preoccupations within schools of architecture, and the world of professional practice has polarised. This split is characterised by a sense that educators find the reality of practice and contingency surrounding the process of building rather mundane, while offices see schools as indulgent, teaching little to prepare young graduates for the challenges ahead. Yet architecture is at a critical point of change that requires a redefinition of working methods and the drivers of practice. To this end, Project Orange initiated an inclusive piece of reflection by asking each studio member to research and write up an area of personal interest with reference to projects they have worked on in the office. The aim was to establish whether a cohesive document could be produced whose authorship was genuinely collective, and which held up a mirror to the studio, bridging the gap between process and academic reflection. The starting point, therefore, was not to try to graft a theory of practice onto the work, but rather to set up a positive dialogue between architects and a wider audience.

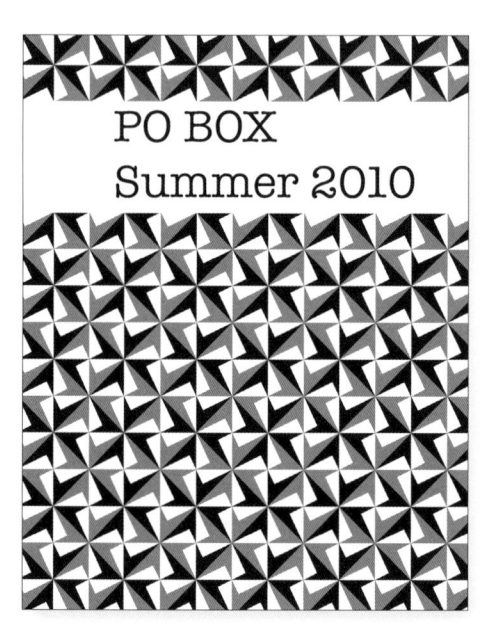

Project Orange,
PO Box 1,
2010

The studio's first research zine, edited by Dr Matthew Barac, was shortlisted for the RIBA President's Award for Research.

Project Orange,
Glasgow School of Art
competition proposal,
2010

A pair of collages is used to explore dynamic spatial relationships in the Glasgow competition bid. While the spatial configurations are ambiguous, the sense of spatial complexity and materiality offers a visceral experience of place.

The Process

The idea for a zine or pamphlet was tabled in 2009 via a presentation to the studio, during which all staff were invited to contribute with open reflections on particular aspects of work they had recently engaged in. Dr Matthew Barac, then a senior lecturer at London South Bank University, was invited to offer guidance, encouragement and academic perspective to the team, while the design of the resulting *PO Box* publication was generated in-house. Initially there was some resistance from staff who saw it as an extracurricular chore and compared it to being back at school again, which in some ways was intentional. However, as the project took shape it became clear that most people were enjoying the task and finding their 'tutorials' with the editor enriching and a valuable tool for their personal development.

PO Box 1

And so we have *PO Box*. Such an impulse to reflect can signal many things; here it indicates an office that is coming of age. On the cusp of maturity Project Orange has begun to get to know itself better.
— Dr Matthew Barac, *PO Box 1* editorial, September 2010

The introduction to *PO Box 1* suggested that Project Orange is not interested in radical theory and does not have a singular mode of practice, but instead sees its projects as narratives or stories, which collected together make a body of work. While this remains true, one essay jumped out as a prescient nudge towards rethinking 'green' issues. In 'The Carrot Versus the Stick', studio member Abi Tuttle argued that the rhetoric around sustainable architecture needed to be recast in a new light; one that is less about technical solutions and more about an understanding of the environment as a whole. Though regulations provide minimum requirements, they hardly inspire the radical change required. Abi's critique of the instrumental 'green machine' movement and appeal for 'cradle-to-cradle' thinking attempt to reconceptualise design as a virtuous circle of materials reuse. The essay is a call for action, and one that Project Orange has taken time to develop, but looking back it is clear this piece of work was an important catalyst in the development of the practice.

In 2011, Project Orange was shortlisted for the RIBA President's Award for Research, up against Foster + Partners and Architecture 00, legitimising the PO Box initiative and demonstrating that small companies can have impact. The project findings were also presented at the 2012 'Theory by Design' conference at the Artesis University College Antwerp, the premise of which was that contemporary architectural theory is typically constructed by academics and within academia with few connections to practice. The sympathetic audience discussion reinforced the intellectual disconnect between established modes of teaching and research and live projects, giving further impetus to the PO Box initiative.

PO Box 2: Questions of Representation

Each piece of text is seen as an opportunity to criticise and understand the nature of representation and the relationship between what is drawn and what is built.
— Jane Tankard, *PO Box 2* editorial, August 2014

During the three-year period since the first research project, the profession had experienced increased demand from clients to produce photoreal renders, a situation brought about by a new wave of tech-savvy graduate employees as well as more powerful software. Uncomfortable with this simulated reality, Project Orange decided to structure *PO Box 2*, edited by Jane Tankard, senior lecturer at the University of Westminster, around the question of representation: What does drawing mean today?

In 'Rules of Representation', team member and architect Emma Elston suggested that architects need to challenge implicit drawing conventions – ideas of perfection, minimal inhabitation and order – and use them instead to reflect a familiar world. She referred to Project Orange's collage approach to drawings that attempt to show a more tangible reality, from sketches to the colour coding in the early concept studies for the four-star Zone Hotels chain the studio designed for the Indian market. The prototype project was built out in Coimbatore, Tamil Nadu, and opened in 2015.

PO Box 2 also revealed that through the process of thinking and writing, the collective continues to nudge, uncover and expose different ways of thinking and designing. Its findings were presented at the Association of Architectural Educators (AAE) conference Living and Learning at the University of Sheffield in 2014, in a paper titled 'Education in Practice'.[3] Despite some seeing the publication as non-academic, conversations between the attendees around how practices can share their own critical positions shaped the direction of the conference. This raised the further issue of disseminating and sharing research; while in academia it is either 'publish or die', practices tend to be very protective of their research, particularly when the outcomes are not overwhelmingly positive, the consequence of which being that learning from other practices is rare.

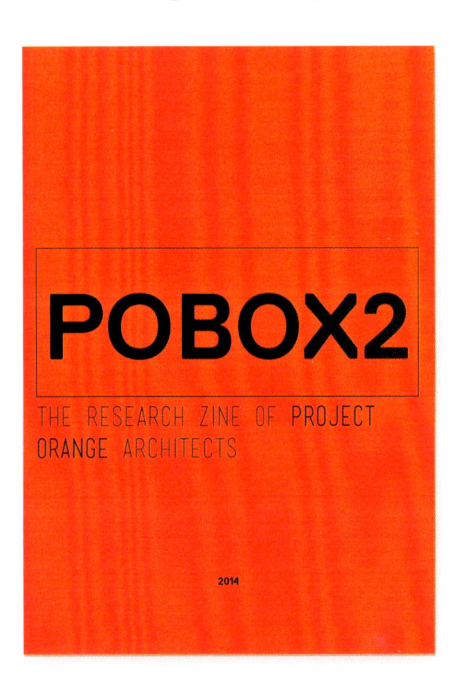

Project Orange,
PO Box 2: Questions of Representation, 2014

Issue 2 chose to explore themes of drawing and representation, reflecting on different modes of communicating.

Project Orange studio,
London,
2016

The team discussing new projects over lunch in the studio.

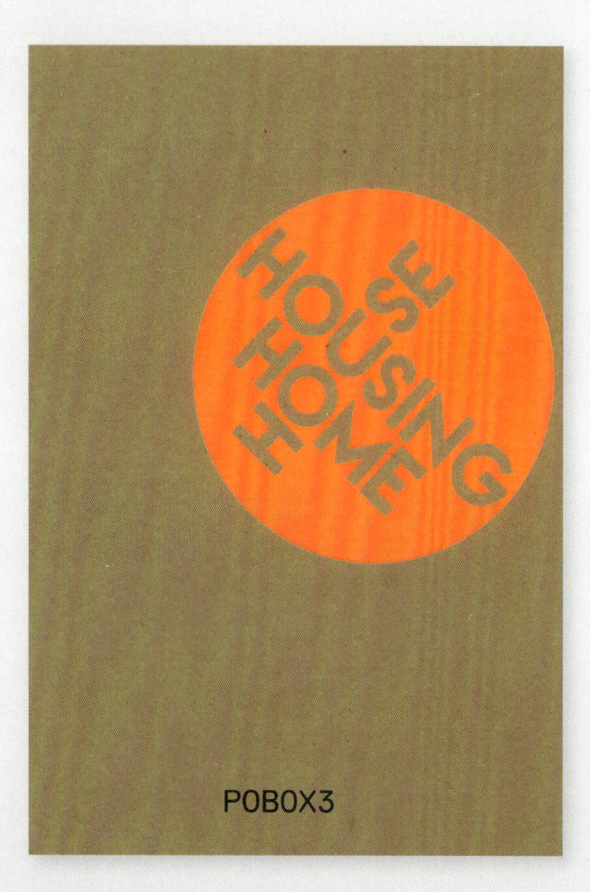

Project Orange,
PO Box 3:
Housing,
House,
Home,
2016

Looking at questions of housing, this issue explored a broad range of themes from design and standards through to societal and ethical concerns.

HOME/WORK

Billy Sinclair

Chapter One

To the untrained eye, this room, where a man sits studiously tapping on a well-worn keyboard, has all the hallmarks of a palatial library. Towering oak bookcases topped with Greek busts line the East wall while three tall French doors take advantage of the westerly light. A pair of Corinthian columns, which serve no purpose but to glamourise the space, frame a central writing desk, where he and his work reside. He looks up momentarily, distracted by the flight of a bird in the afternoon light, before returning to his studious tapping. The only other audible volume is the muffled rattle of pages being fed through a concealed printer, the day's work crystallised on paper. The man pulls a cigarette out of the top drawer of the desk, lights it and removes his tortoise-shell glasses. Closing his eyes for a moment of distilled silence, he then exhales smoke in a long easy action. This figure has the appearance of a man who has perfectly imitated the image of luxury.

'Mr Wilson…Mr Wilson!' a shrill voice and knocking from the only internal door in the room instantly kills the peace.
'Yes?'
'Mr Wilson, err, a Mr Samuels is here to see you'
'Send him up'
Feet are heard hurrying down the stone staircase. Wilson stubs out the cigarette, closes the lid of his laptop and turns to open one of the French doors. Footsteps return, this time in a more collective manner, and the door swings open to present a small plump lady followed by an even more plump man dressed in a pinstriped suit.

'Tom, good to see you, good to see you old boy!' Wilson announces jovially.
'Wilson, how the heck are you?' a wry smile appearing from a well-tanned round face.
'Good, very good.' Wilson takes Tom's hand with a firm grasp, as the door closes behind them.
'This is quite the place you've got here Wilson.' Tom says, looking round the room.
Wilson acknowledges the compliment with a smile. 'Take a seat,' hand raised towards the armchairs that address the fireplace. 'What can I get you?'
'What's the time?'

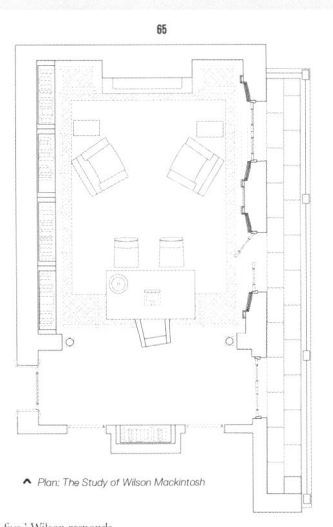

> A fictional conversation in two parts, the piece, entitled 'Home/Work', highlights the differences between clients with money, where design is only about delight, and those with fewer choices where design is presented as a negotiation with minimum standards and resources

Plan: The Study of Wilson Mackintosh

PO Box 3: Housing, House, Home

> PO Box is not just about starting focused conversations but poking the beast, irritating the oyster, cultivating unique thought and expression from their mighty young workforce.
> — Gem Barton, *PO Box 3* editorial, July 2016

PO Box 3 was developed during the first operating year of the London School of Architecture (LSA) and the school's agenda is clearly reflected in the ambition of the publication. Staff were here encouraged to think about the housing crisis, architects' agency, and whether the profession is in some ways complicit. The most original piece of writing came out of conversations between Project Orange architect Billy Sinclair and editor Gem Barton, who encourages new forms of creative writing within architectural discourse at the University of Brighton. A fictional conversation in two parts, the piece, entitled 'Home/Work', highlights the differences between clients with money, where design is only about delight, and those with fewer choices where design is presented as a negotiation with minimum standards and resources. It cleverly draws attention to the conflicted role of architects in the context of homemaking.

Community of Practice

Encompassing both writing and reflection, the *PO Box* research project has flowed into 'Critical Practice' teaching at the LSA, where instead of producing a cookie-cutter dissertation, students are invited to develop a manifesto for their future selves. A number of students reflected in their course feedback that writing the manifesto gave them permission to spend focused time sorting their thoughts about architecture and to ask themselves where they see their own trajectories and values.

What began as an experiment is now embedded within the studio's culture, and the fourth issue on the 'Value of Architecture' is underway. Perhaps the most significant outcome is that it reflects an approach that follows Carlo Ratti's idea of the 'choral' architect[4] – working together as a team whose thinking is fully accessible and open source to generate new research out of practice.

Notes
1. Reinier de Graaf, 'Architecture is Now a Tool of Capital', *Architectural Review*, 1419, May 2015, p 43.
2. 'RIBA CPD Core Curriculum'; www.architecture.com/education-cpd-and-careers/cpd/cpd-core-curriculum.
3. James Soane, 'Education in Practice', Living and Learning: 2nd International Conference of the Association of Architectural Educators (AAE), University of Sheffield, 3–5 September 2014.
4. Carlo Ratti, *Open Source Architecture*, Thames & Hudson (London), 2015, p 120.

Billy Sinclair/
Project Orange,
'Home/Work',
PO Box 3,
2016

Opening spread showing the study plan of Sinclair's fictional character in his 'Home/Work' essay for *PO Box 3*.

Text © 2019 John Wiley & Sons Ltd. Images: pp 48-51, 52(bl), 52-3(b) © Project Orange; p 52(t) © Project Orange, photo Alex Sarginson

Anab Jain, Jon Ardern and Danielle Knight

Mitigation of Shock

Post-Occupancy

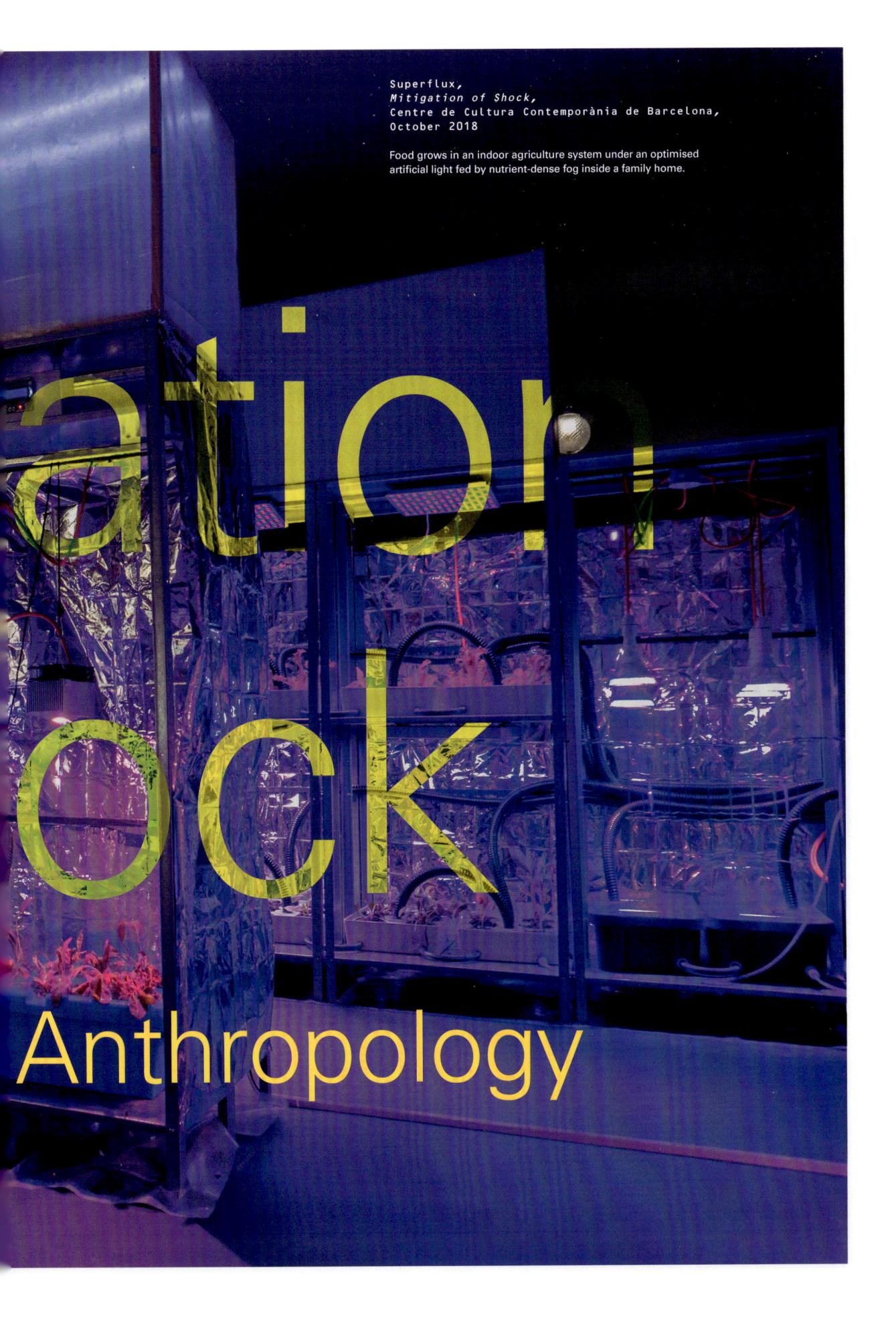

Superflux,
Mitigation of Shock,
Centre de Cultura Contemporània de Barcelona,
October 2018

Food grows in an indoor agriculture system under an optimised artificial light fed by nutrient-dense fog inside a family home.

Getting people truly on board requires not just intellectual explanations, but emotional connection. So how can the need to address climate change be made real to the average urbanite? By creating an immersive experience of a city apartment as it might look in 2050, London design studio Superflux's installation *Mitigation of Shock* confronts us with the likely impact of global warming on the way we live, while offering insights that we could apply to take control of our destinies. Here, studio co-founders **Anab Jain and Jon Ardern**, and studio researcher **Danielle Knight**, describe the design research process that produced it, from interviews with specialists in a broad range of fields to materials investigations and prototyping.

Architecture and utopianism are understandable bedfellows. Both are future-oriented, driven by a desire for a better place for living and being. Architecture reaches beyond this desire, to realise visions of a better place in concrete form. Roland Barthes remarked: 'Architecture is always dream and function, expression of utopia and instrument of convenience.'[1]

Today, architects must often navigate the increasing complexity of regulations, tightening budgets, and fast-shifting sociocultural conditions. Architectural research takes place within these constraints and under many different guises, ranging from the design process itself as research, to theoretical and cultural research. Yet the need to balance conceptual vision with the functionality of a space, place or building remain; both are shaped by the architectural research underpinning the project.

Speculative Design

The touring installation *Mitigation of Shock* by speculative design studio Superflux transports visitors to a fictional future living space in 2050, where the West has moved from material abundance to scarcity. This possible future is blighted by extreme weather conditions caused by climate change, where global supply chains have faltered. Everyday items are regularly out of stock or have become expensive luxuries. The installation uses speculative design to give members of the public insight into the lived experience of this possible world. Superflux's work defines possible problems, before designing potential solutions. For *Mitigation of Shock* this involved defining the problems invoked by a world marred by climate change, before designing a domestic space around a lifestyle where consumer items are no longer readily available.

Stretching the Idea of Architectural Research

What might architectural practice look like if the sociocultural environment disrupts this balance between dream and function? What does architectural research look like when designing a future living space which is built in the present? What does utopian expression look like under these constraints?

Kitchen shelves are stocked with books for cooking in times of scarcity, including titles such as 'Pets as Protein'. The intricate details from speculative artefacts like these activate visitors' imaginations about what living with less might be like.

The installation featured a life-size simulation of a speculative apartment in London in the year 2050.

Superflux are known for deconstructing the polarity of utopian and dystopian imagining to build and explore complex, heterogeneous futures which can be experienced in the present. Their two-pronged, hybrid practice operates at the intersection between foresight and speculative design. Like much architectural research, their investigations are often embedded within the practice itself, but their foresight approach clearly differentiates their work. Architecture commonly deals with immediate or near-term futures. Superflux's work necessitates imagining another place and time, in a medium-term future very different from today.

Foresight and Materials Investigation

Foresight and materials investigation define the studio's practice. Envisioning the 2050 world of *Mitigation of Shock* was grounded in considerable desk research accompanied by in-depth interviews with climate-change experts at NASA, the UK Met Office, MIT Media Lab and Forum for the Future and independent professionals from the fields of biotechnology, social science, agriculture and economics. Rigorous foresight depends on rigorous sources, and these methods of data collection informed the subsequent horizon scanning and trend extrapolation process. Superflux were then able to construct a data-grounded vision of a world where the threat from climate change had been largely ignored and human behaviour had remained the same.

From this foundation, Superflux launched into the materials investigation strand of their work through an exploration

> Superflux are known for deconstructing the polarity of utopian and dystopian imagining to build and explore complex, heterogeneous futures

The mycelium: mushrooms thrive in a domestic environment optimised by food computers, created by the speculative design laboratory Superflux.

View from the window into the outside world of London in 2050 from the *Mitigation of Shock* apartment.

In the living area, a newspaper dated in the year 2050 reporting worldwide crop failures is discarded on a coffee table next to the remnants of breakfast and a child's toy.

into the domestic needs and requirements of inhabitants living this future. Their foresight strategy raised the question of domestic lived experience in this possible world, and revealed that domestic DIY food production would be a major priority. It was evident that the architectural balancing act between dreaming and functionality in this context would fall in favour of functionality. By combining foresight with materials investigation and live prototyping methodology, the team researched different possible solutions to the problem of cultivating sustenance in the home.

A Live Prototyping Methodology

Technologists from Superflux experimented with cheap or scavenged materials to develop alternative food systems. Food-growing apparatus for the earliest prototypes was salvaged from discarded materials found around Bermondsey in South London, before sturdier, accessible alternatives were identified. Initially, the team carried out small food-growing experiments, before scaling up to test efficiency. Many plants died or drowned. At one point, a faulty fogponics system flooded the laboratory. Eventually, towering silver stacks of mushrooms, cabbages and chilli plants began to flourish in an optimally lit indoor environment, with plants sustained by temperature-controlled, nutrient-dense fog. Green, bubbling spirulina tanks thrived, glowing alongside a mealworm farm.

The Immersive Experience

In the final installation, echoes of the anticipated utopia of the smart home and automated living were bathed in the eerie purple light of an experimental domestic agriculture system powered by DIY food computers and fogponics. Visitors were able to sit down on a familiar IKEA sofa and experience the feeling of living amongst the blasted ruins of capitalism. Superflux's purpose was ultimately anthropological: to immerse people within a simulated living space to help them understand the reality of constantly adapting one's home in response to shifting external conditions. Although being immersed in this uncanny environment might initially feel dystopian, Superflux intended visitors to leave feeling hopeful. By inventing speculative food-computer prototypes from salvaged materials – which successfully grow produce indoors – living with climate change becomes prescient and tangible, yet surmountable. Strange yet familiar worlds like *Mitigation of Shock* give experiential and emotional insights into likely challenges on the horizon, but also propose solutions for mitigating against them. ⌑

Note
1. Roland Barthes, 'The Eiffel Tower', in Neil Leach (ed), *Rethinking Architecture: A Reader in Cultural Theory*, Routledge (London), 1997, p 174.

Strange yet familiar worlds like *Mitigation of Shock* give experiential and emotional insights into likely challenges on the horizon, but also propose solutions for mitigating against them

Text © 2019 John Wiley & Sons Ltd. Images © Anab Jain, Superflux

Ziona Strelitz

How Is It For You?

Grafton Architects,
LSE Marshall Building,
London,
due for completion 2021

Extending the School's ambitious campus development, the construction programme for this new building addressing Lincoln's Inn Fields follows close behind another major new LSE building on site in Houghton Street. LSE Estates' objective in commissioning ZZA to undertake process evaluations during these projects' design and construction life is to learn lessons for future procurement.

Building Design as Experienced by Users and Makers

Effective evaluation of architectural schemes – whether in progress or completed – can generate evidence and action to enhance people's experience of buildings and spaces. **Ziona Strelitz**, founding director of London-based specialists ZZA Responsive User Environments, advocates 'design anthropology', an approach she has developed and honed to join meaningful dots in understanding the interplay of the myriad elements that define built spaces and influence their use. Emphasising the benefits of in-depth, in-situ, structured interviews over online surveys, she describes three main modes of research, with examples of her practice's contribution across a wide range of users and building types – governmental, academic, banking, media, commercial, policing and public realm.

Many types of research have a role in informing built-environment design. Unlike the vast field of technical research on components, structures and materials, the studies undertaken by ZZA Responsive User Environments sit at the intersection of built space and people. Grounded in social anthropology, and deeply conversant with design disciplines at all spatial scales, this distinctive combination of expertise is essentially design anthropology. Its methods comprise relevant framing, skilled questioning, experienced listening and attuned observing, all informing – and then joining up – the great number of socio-spatial dots involved in the use of any built space. Importantly, as research that is independent of design creation, it is free from bias on both what works well and potential alternatives. Enriched by cumulative learning, it leverages a wider repertoire of knowledge than that generated by any single study – to set the agenda, enlist pertinent references in interpreting findings, and register cultural change.

ZZA's research on the social aspects of design involves three main modes. The first comprises contextual studies on changing culture. Driven by forces such as technology, globalisation and demographics, changing context shapes how we use space and provisions to accommodate evolving uses. The second mode focuses on how 'users' perceive and experience physical settings, through briefing research to inform projects before they are built, and as post-occupancy evaluation (POE) to 'test' settings that have been delivered. The third, research with project contributors, focuses on human agency in built outcomes.

Changing Culture
Informing purpose is a rational starting point for design. Recognising social trends and their implications for built space can strengthen design, both technically and typologically. The following examples from ZZA's research show how and why this can matter.

To position a group of speculative office buildings – on what became Leeds City Office Park in the 1990s – as usefully innovative and meeting market acceptance, the practice researched local perspectives on commercial accommodation. The first 20 structured interviews with business leaders generated precepts for the new buildings, which a second 20 tested for acceptability. A pivot was low-energy design, to which the client – commencing a programme to develop obsolete gas sites – was committed, and for which the strategy of the architects, Foggo Associates, was based on exposed concrete mass and night purging. In parallel, the research identified a notable regional presence of call centres – then a relatively new business (and building) typology, contingent on information technology (IT), and frequently operating round the clock – a use that would conflict with the proposed approach to service the building. In the event, a mobile telecommunications provider took the space, seeking its fine spatial quality to support its performance in customer care. As the centre operated 24 hours a day, the occupier installed conspicuous supplementary cooling plant on the roof and floors. While one can never mitigate against all risk, acting on relevant research knowledge can help avoid such outcomes.

A more macro contextual example relates to IT dissemination, enabling people to work untethered to organisations or fixed locations. In 2011, the workplace provider Regus commissioned ZZA to undertake an international study to identify the factors underlying work in 'third places' (neither designated places of employment nor homes). Focusing on where people with choice choose to work, ZZA carried out 86 in-depth interviews in business centres, library and cafe settings in city centres and outer zones of big metropolitan areas. Reinforced by 17,800 responses to ZZA questions in an online global questionnaire, the study identified two primary attractors to working in these venues: accessible to but away from home, and being galvanised by others who are also working. Since publication of the related report, titled *Why Place Still Matters in the Digital Age*,[1] the growth of workplace hubs and co-working spaces has mushroomed, affording vast new user choice in character and locality. The expanded scope both for outer locations, and to recycle existing buildings, represents significant design opportunities identified by research.

Buildings as Experienced Settings
The rationale for learning from building users is 'the eye of the beholder'. That the giver's view is not inevitably the receiver's is certainly true for design. Forging a proposition from myriad – almost infinite – possibilities, designers see their creation with conviction, whereas users experience the resultant spaces with a different salience, as settings they occupy in a sequence of intended or incidental locales.

The ubiquitous assertion that architecture's purpose is supporting use is often flouted by designers' complaint that 'the users don't understand the design', 'don't appreciate it', 'don't know how to use it'. This often references earlier designs that were controversial when delivered, though validated years later. In contrast, ZZA's practice objective is to inform design for effective contemporary use, through briefing research and POE. Both study how people perceive and experience existing settings.

ZZA's briefing research for the fit-out of the British Broadcasting Company's (BBC's) Media Centre at White City in London (2004, base build by architects Allies and Morrison) followed the Director-General's mandate to BBC Property for all staff to have a say in defining their workspace. To fulfil this at the organisation's large scale, ZZA researched individual preferences on a suite of loose-fit elements, to apply in neighbourhood solutions that offered functional relevance and expressed team identity, with coherence across the interior.

POE, the second form of structured learning from users, 'tests' settings that are already built. The cumbersome term is the least of its issues; the wide range of drivers is more important for practice. With increasing pressure for teams to commission or undertake POE – including as specified under Stage 7 in the Royal Institute of British Architects' (RIBA's) Plan of Work[2] – intent ranges from 'box-ticking' to comply with requirements, or 'a foot in the door' to re-start dialogue with a client, through 'benchmarking' to demonstrate a project's comparative merits, to understanding the multiple design interfaces that impinge on users' spatial experience. With ZZA's clients wanting specialist independent research on the effectiveness of their designs for users, all of the practice's POEs have addressed the latter. Most of these have been commissions by developers and occupiers, but also by architects, including Grimshaw Architects' Global Technology Centre in Southampton for Lloyd's Register of Shipping (2014), and Make Architects' 65,300-square-metre (703,000-square-foot) building for investment bank UBS at 5 Broadgate, London (2016), designed for 6,000 occupants. Post-occupancy research can feed into future briefing: ZZA's POEs of the BBC Media and Broadcast Centres at White City in London helped inform the fit-out brief for BBC Scotland's subsequent building at Pacific Quay, Glasgow (2007, by David Chipperfield). ZZA had previously done briefing research with users in the BBC's former Glasgow workspace in Queen Margaret's Drive to inform the design competition for the building.

```
Make Architects,
5 Broadgate,
London,
2015
```

In August 2018, two years after the building's phased occupancy, the architects commissioned ZZA to undertake an independent POE study. This research involved systematic, structured interviews to enlist thoughtful responses from a cross-section of occupants, all employees of the large international bank to whose brief the 13-storey, stainless-steel-clad building was designed.

The expanded scope both for outer locations, and to recycle existing buildings, represents significant design opportunities identified by research

How We Learn from Users

There is wide variation in ways to capture user experience. Approaches range from self-completion questionnaires to neurological testing. In a field that is patently prone to subjectivity, the latter's apparent alignment with clinical science exerts some cachet, despite referencing limited impacts of design. ZZA's comparative research on methods does demonstrate the 'softness' of user research. When the same questions are addressed to a building population in face-to-face interviews or online, the profiles of response differ; the tendency in interviews is for users to be more considered.

ZZA's ethnographic and holistic approach favours systematic interviews, in situ, with samples of users representing both the range of building conditions – floors, zones and orientations – and the different capacities in which they are used. Interviews provide for engagement with users, explanation of their reasoning, and opportunities to observe, all affording a more informative picture than can be gleaned from online responses – typically given in isolation and disassociated from specified parts of the building.

Enric Miralles,
Scottish Parliament,
Holyrood,
Edinburgh,
2004

below: The signature architecture for the Scottish Parliament, as manifested here in the roof of the garden lobby, responded to the briefing objective to attract attention to the new institution. The building's effectiveness in meeting this aim generated consistently large numbers of visitors for the Facilities Management team to support.

above: The building's character as an actual ensemble, seen in this aerial view, gives rise to complexity. ZZA's research engaged with the Facilities Management team, as specialist users whose particular knowledge offers important learning on functionality.

What We Learn

Research also differs in the way questions are framed. Some surveys lead to positive answers, and some questions – like 'Were you happy in the building?' – have tenuous capacity to shed light on design. However, there is typical content across building use studies, covering thermal, lighting and acoustic experience, circulation, space, image and durability – either as synoptic headlines, or with more granulation. The trade-offs are between time (researchers' and respondents'), budget for data capture and analysis, and richness of information. ZZA includes a greater range of elements, expanding the scope to learn about influences and interactions between them.

The content can involve the same questions to all users, or adaptations for distinctive types of use. ZZA's evaluation of the Scottish Parliament building in Edinburgh (2004, by Enric Miralles) focused on people running the space and its services, to learn from their experience of the design's facilitation and constraints. The research evidenced the building's capacity to be run effectively, at high standards of sustainable practice. Given its reputed complexity, and the many visitors attracted by its architecture (which was intended to stimulate interest in the Parliament), the findings endorsed both the building design and management.

Scale, too, is relevant to content. Is one studying a building, a fit-out or a campus? Whilst few users differentiate aspects of their setting as fixed or loose-fit, built or managed, instructive research distinguishes these layers and their respective impacts. ZZA's POEs of the BBC's buildings at the White City Media Village separated the effects of the base build and fit-out. Whilst the latter provided numerous 'sparky' settings to promote interaction between co-locating departments, the research pointed to the strong influence of the linear plan, punctuated by three full-height atria. ZZA's POEs at the Chiswick Park office development (phased development commenced 1999, completed 2016; by Rogers Stirk Harbour + Partners) distinguished the site's masterplan from its base build design in shaping user experience. Whilst people appreciated the buildings' clear heights and full perimeter glazing, the research was most definitive in affirming the visionary site arrangement that restricts vehicles to the perimeter zone, and created a compelling, pedestrian-only, central landscaped oasis. Standardised research with generic content would eclipse such learning.

Rogers Stirk Harbour + Partners,
Chiswick Park office development,
London, 1999–2016

above: In restricting vehicular circulation to the zone around the rear of the office buildings, the masterplan – audacious for a speculative office campus – enabled a large pedestrianised open space, including this fine soft-landscaped linear oasis. ZZA's POE showed users' effusion in their appreciation and enjoyment of this amenity.

below: By concentrating the space between the buildings in the centre of the site, the arrangement also provides a valuable hard-landscaped area, for sports, events and relaxation.

Grimshaw Architects,
LSE New Academic Building,
London,
2008

ZZA's approach to the briefing for this bespoke LSE building behind a retained facade was to widen the user benefits beyond academic offices and teaching space alone. The resultant accommodation includes cafes, scope for public engagement, outdoor terraces, and informal study and gathering space – some in the central atrium, with its signature timber 'sounding board', active perimeter spaces and excellent daylight.

Utility

With the variable approaches described, what value could there be in publishing POE data in the public domain? There is not just lack of comparability contingent on research methods, significant though this is. POE is also a temporal snapshot – the phenomena change, both independently of the research and as an outcome of it. ZZA's first POE at Chiswick Park in 2006 heard numerous comments on available car-parking. In another evaluation two years later, only one user made this point. The provision had not changed; London's congestion charge had bedded down in the interim, and commuting by car had faded from expectations.

Change also results from research. Every ZZA evaluation – including the highest achieving – has generated an action agenda to enhance user experience, and study following implementation shows increased user satisfaction. Indeed, most ZZA studies are commissioned by repeat procurers, who look to apply the learning on subsequent schemes. A series of POEs for London's Metropolitan Police offers a pithy example. Whereas the first three custody centres evaluated in 2011 and 2012 were solid volumes, the fourth, evaluated in 2013, had a skylight above the custody desk. The client related this to ZZA's initial POE report, which prompted a change in the client organisation's brief, to admit daylight and external aspect to development that was then in the pipeline. Strategic use of research is also well exemplified by the London School of Economics (LSE), for whom ZZA has undertaken serial user studies pertaining to new buildings, adapted buildings, interiors, the campus, and settings like library and study space. Starting with briefing research to inform the New Academic Building (2008, by Grimshaw Architects), an explicit line of progression is discernible across this body of research – with the outputs of each study informing subsequent briefs and designs. A chapter on ZZA's POE of the School's Saw Swee Hock Student Centre (2014, by O'Donnell + Tuomey) is included in the monograph on the building.[3]

Learning on user experience can also be transmitted through expert review. ZZA's pre-evaluation of the White Collar Factory in London (2017, by AHMM) encompassed 580 discrete questions, covering different user groups and spatial scales. ZZA has repeated the methodology in other commissions by the developer Derwent London to pre-evaluate their large-scale schemes at 80 Charlotte Street (due for completion 2020, by Make Architects), and the Brunel Building in Paddington (due for completion 2019, by Fletcher Priest Architects). A key point is to optimise timing – sufficiently advanced for there to be substantive design to interrogate; not too advanced to limit scope to adapt.

Researching Human Agency in Project Evolution
All designs are exposed to translation in implementation, and every project team encounters specific challenges that recede from focus when it disbands. Process evaluation – research on design conception and realisation – can identify strengths and risks to inform future delivery. Recent ZZA process evaluations include those for a new student centre building at the University of the West of England in Bristol (2015, by Stride Treglown) at the post-occupancy stage, and RIBA Stages 0–4 of the Marshall Building for the LSE (due for completion 2021, by Grafton Architects) prior to construction.

To enlist useful, open appraisal from contributors, it is crucial that they trust that the client champions good design. ZZA's record of independent research commissions points to a solid and growing client constituency who are giving evidence-based design meaning in action. Ð

Notes
1. Ziona Strelitz, *Why Place Still Matters in the Digital Age: Third Place Working in Easy Reach of Home*, 2011; www.zza.co.uk/resources/Why_Place_Still_Matters_in_the_Digital_Age_ZZA.pdf.
2. See RIBA Plan of Work website: https://www.ribaplanofwork.com.
3. Ziona Strelitz, 'Post Occupancy Review', in Julian S Robinson (ed), *Saw Swee Hock: The Realisation of the London School of Economics Student Centre*, Artifice (London), 2015, pp 108–17.

Text © 2019 John Wiley & Sons Ltd. Images: pp 60-61 © Grafton Architects; p 63 © Make Architects; p 64 Images © Scottish Parliamentary Corporate Body; p 65 © ZZA Responsive User Environments; pp 66-7 © Grimshaw Architects/Dee Dee Lim

Daniel Davis

Vertically Integrated Research

An Unusual Business Model

WeWork,
Chelsea, New York,
2018

In WeWork's global headquarters, designers regularly test out different work environments. The impact of these new spaces is assessed by WeWork's workplace strategy team using a combination of observations, interviews and sensor data.

WeWork designs, constructs and manages offices around the globe that serve as a unique test bed through close ongoing contact with their users. Founded in New York in 2010, it is one of the world's fastest-growing companies, now with over 335 offices that each contain similar elements but combine them in slightly different ways. **Daniel Davis**, a Director of Research at the firm, here explains how their similarity allows his team to pinpoint the subtle reasons for differences in performance – from desk placement to the impact of staircases on social networks – and to feed this back into new projects, boosting both the occupants' experience and the company's success.

Architects rarely get the opportunity to systematically analyse the consequences of their design decisions. 'Because our heuristic seems to be "Never look back", we are unable to predict the longer term consequences of what we design,' writes Frank Duffy.[1] Given that buildings cost millions of dollars, consume vast quantities of resources, and greatly impact people's overall happiness and productivity, it seems odd that designers so rarely return to past projects in order to learn from past successes and mistakes. This dearth of research could be attributed to many things – a lack of money, tools or motivation – but fundamentally it is the industry's business model that seems to inhibit architects from more regularly studying past work.

WeWork has a different business model from most architecture firms. At the core of WeWork's business, its team designs spaces, constructs them, and rents them out for a monthly fee. In effect, WeWork is a vertically integrated company, with design, construction, sales and building operations all performed in-house rather than being contracted to separate entities.

WeWork's organisational structure may seem like an implementation detail more pertinent to businesspeople than to researchers, but it is a critical detail since the structure of a business impacts the value of research. At WeWork, business and research are intertwined – you cannot have one without the other. In particular, there are three aspects of WeWork's research that depend on its vertical integration: (1) being able to rapidly contact thousands of users; (2) being able to generalise research findings across a portfolio of related projects; (3) being held financially accountable to the performance of design concepts. By understanding how business structures enable research, it may be possible to overcome some of the barriers that architects encounter when trying to integrate research into their practice.

WeWork,
Dalian Lu, Shanghai,
2018

Most WeWork locations feature a similar combination of programmatic elements. In this Shanghai location, a lounge space is framed by a row of meeting rooms (left) and a communal kitchen (right).

WeWork,
Houston Galleria,
Houston, Texas,
2018

To the left is an example of WeWork's conversation rooms, a type of meeting room that was developed in response to research showing that most meetings at WeWork did not suit large, formal presentation facilities but instead involved one to four people talking to each other.

WeWork is a vertically integrated company, with design, construction, sales and building operations all performed in-house rather than being contracted to separate entities

Knowing the User

If you do not know who uses your project, you cannot study how your design choices affect them. Designers may have hunches or intuitions, but you need to get in there and observe or interview people to truly understand what is happening in the space.

For many architects, the end-user is something of a mystery – an anonymous person separated by layers of intermediaries. These intermediaries naturally arise as the project passes through the many entities typically involved (the architect hands the design to a contractor, who delivers it to a developer, who gives it to a broker, who sells or rents it to the end-user). By the end of this process, the user is so many times removed from the architect that the architect normally does not know the inhabitant's name, let alone anything about how they are using the space. Even in the best-case scenario, where the client is also the end-user, the architect meets with the client early in the process but it is rare that a client wants to continue seeing the architect after the space is completed. Thus architects more often than not find themselves on the other side of the walls they build, unsure of what is happening behind closed doors.

A staircase linking a communal lounge and kitchen at WeLive. Research shows that these staircases increase the likelihood of residents being friends with one another.

```
WeLive,
Crystal City, Virginia,
2016
```

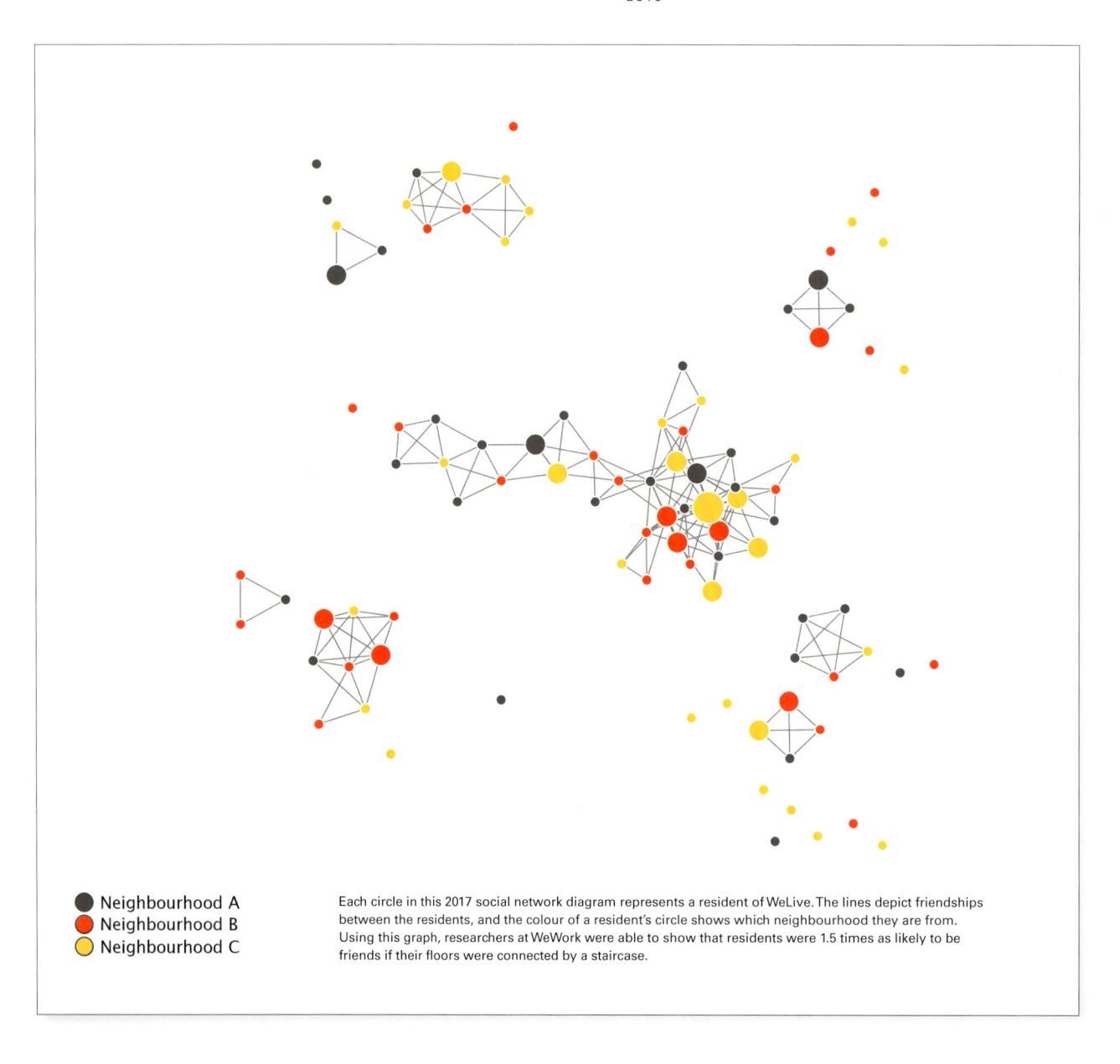

- Neighbourhood A
- Neighbourhood B
- Neighbourhood C

Each circle in this 2017 social network diagram represents a resident of WeLive. The lines depict friendships between the residents, and the colour of a resident's circle shows which neighbourhood they are from. Using this graph, researchers at WeWork were able to show that residents were 1.5 times as likely to be friends if their floors were connected by a staircase.

There are, of course, instances where researchers have gained access to people in private spaces. Leon Festinger studied students in college dorms,[2] Jeanne Arnold et al created an intimate portrait of families living in LA,[3] and a small number of architecture firms revisit their buildings to conduct post-occupancy evaluations.[4] But these studies are the exception. Most of the research on people interacting with the built environment takes place in public spaces where people are more easily observed and where the disconnect between the architect and the user is not as pronounced (think: Jane Jacobs's observations of great American cities,[5] William Whyte's studies of pedestrians in New York,[6] and Jan Gehl's research on the life between buildings[7]).

WeWork knows all the people using its spaces. There are no particularly sophisticated tools or tricks to gain access to these people. Instead, it is simply a byproduct of WeWork's business model. Since WeWork is both the designer and the owner of their spaces, there are no intermediaries between WeWork and the people using the spaces – the members pay WeWork directly and WeWork is entirely responsible for these members' experience.

Compared to the advances that other researchers are making with algorithms, data models and related technologies, knowing an inhabitant's name and email address may seem like an insignificant development. But for researchers at WeWork, knowing the user of a space enables a type of investigation that would be unimaginable in a typical architectural setting. Researchers have, for instance, studied the emotional impact of aesthetic choices by surveying tens of thousands of people in hundreds of different work settings. They have asked people from around the world to take photographs of their desks, of their lunch and of their favourite workplace, which has produced an intimate glimpse of workplaces in different cultures. They have interviewed dozens of new mothers about their experiences using lactation rooms. And they have asked people to name their closest work friends in order to understand how spatial decisions impact social networks (a revised version of Festinger's seminal dorm-room study[8]). It is incredibly useful information for designers that becomes easy to gather once you know the names of the people using your spaces.

The Hidden Cost of Originality
Another challenge of studying the built environment is that every building is unique, which makes it difficult to use findings from one project to the next. That is to say, even if you learn something insightful on one project, it's not always clear whether these lessons will translate to a new building with a different client, a different site, a different layout and a different programme.

This has become especially difficult in recent years, with a number of architects showing a stylistic aversion to anything that is repetitive. Taken to its logical extreme, they have discarded regular construction modules in favour of parametrically derived shapes where every element is unique. The result is an expanding collection of bespoke buildings where every floor, window and column is itself bespoke, one-off and original. All of this novelty has a hidden cost: in a world where every building is unique, and every variable is in play, it becomes increasingly difficult to find commonalities and truths that are applicable to future projects.

Each WeWork location is a unique design specific to the site conditions and the local culture. The designs are created by a team of interior designers, architects, engineers, artists and other specialists who follow a global style guide that they modify to fit the local context. With over 335 locations open, the result is a collection of buildings that each have their own personality while sharing a common DNA. These buildings are similar enough to compare to one another but different enough to learn from each of them.

In a recent project, researchers at WeWork attempted to predict which offices would be the most difficult to rent. The designers at WeWork suspected that rooms with windows would presumably be easier to rent and that rooms beside bathrooms or with awkward internal columns might be harder to rent. The researchers analysed the spatial features of thousands of offices in the WeWork portfolio and combined these with sales data for each room. Applying a form of machine learning called support vector classification, the researchers were able to determine, with around 60–70 per cent accuracy, the spatial features of an office that makes it difficult to rent.[9] WeWork's revenue optimisation team then incorporated the most salient features into their pricing model, allowing WeWork to identify, price and remedy poorly performing offices before they are constructed.

`WeWork,`
`WeWork portfolio,`
`2018`

80 floorplates from the hundreds of buildings in WeWork's portfolio. These buildings are similar enough to compare but different enough to have a variety of outcomes, providing researchers with a Petri dish of locations to study.

Even if you learn something insightful on one project, it's not always clear whether these lessons will translate to a new building with a different client, a different site, a different layout and a different programme

Comparing thousands of offices would not be possible if they all had unique furniture, finishes and layouts. Because the WeWork offices follow a common design language, they have enough similarity to make this type of research viable. The researchers can also be confident that their results are generalisable since they are observing these patterns in dozens of buildings rather than taking anecdotal lessons from individual projects. In many ways, this requires thinking more pluralistically about projects – instead of treating every project as an individual experiment, it is a portfolio of projects that become the experiment.

Skin in the Game

In many respects, architects are paid to look forward, to imagine what our cities might look like many years into the future. They are rarely paid to look back.

The make-or-break point for any architect comes early in the project. The architect has to convince the client (whether through a competition, a bid or just a lot of charm) that their vision of the future is worth building. Beyond this point, unless something goes catastrophically wrong, they have limited financial exposure to the success of the project – just look at the number of projects that run over budget and behind schedule.[10]

Because WeWork is vertically integrated, if a project is delivered over budget, WeWork is liable for the expense. If a project is delivered late, WeWork has to rehouse hundreds of people who were expecting it to be open. And if a project does not perform as expected, WeWork is stuck with offices that are difficult to rent.

Since WeWork's business depends on consistently delivering high-performing projects, its employees are naturally invested in the outcome of their work. Quite often architects and designers conduct their own investigations, gathering data on how particular spaces are used, analysing feedback they have received, talking to people running locations, and walking through projects making their own observations about how people are using the space. These are not necessarily formal research projects, but there is a culture of curiosity and experimentation. Just like any other research project at WeWork, these informal studies benefit immensely from being able to contact users and to generalise findings across a portfolio of related projects.

Given the hunger for performance, people at WeWork are generally receptive of research. The research is typically distributed to teams working on design standards, design processes and the creative direction, which then makes its way into the wider design process. The research is also shared with other employees in the form of written reports, presentations, a newsletter and a podcast. At times researchers encounter impediments that are common at large companies – sometimes the business moves faster than the researchers, sometimes researchers study the wrong thing, or find nothing of interest, or find that it is too expensive to implement findings. At times, researchers have also found themselves under a lot of pressure given the high-stakes nature of WeWork's vertical integration (in an academic context, a mistake may be caught by a peer reviewer a few months later, but at WeWork the research is applied almost immediately and any mistake can have real consequences). Despite all of this, WeWork's researchers have influenced everything from the design of lactation rooms to the placement of stairs, the function of office furniture and the quantity of meeting rooms. It is research that happens primarily because WeWork's business model makes everyone invested in the performance of the projects.

WeWork, WeWork office metrics, 2017

Examples of room features that were used to help predict the difficulty of renting a given office. This data was extracted from BIM data produced as part of the modelling process for every project.

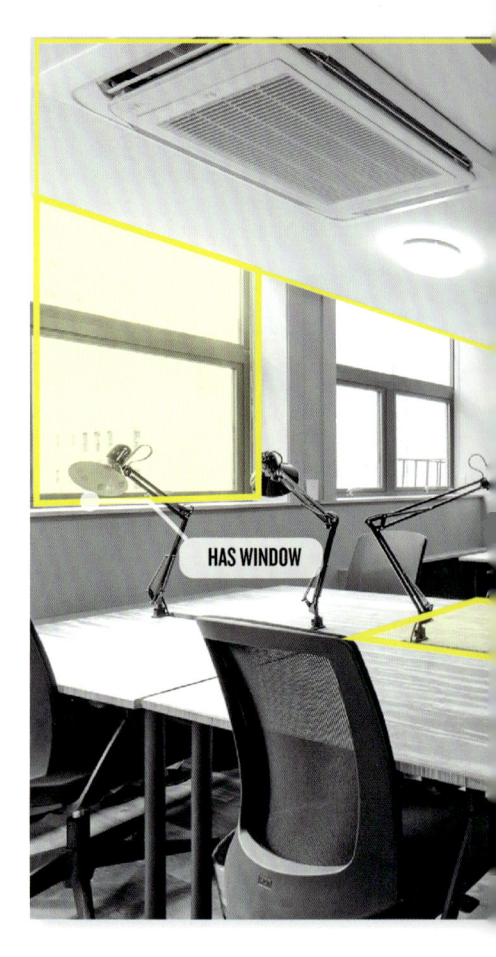

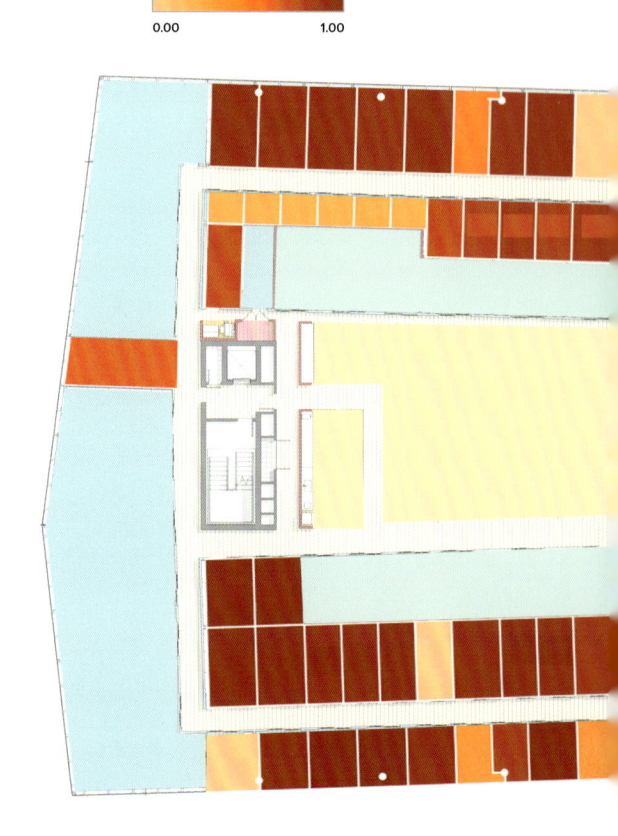

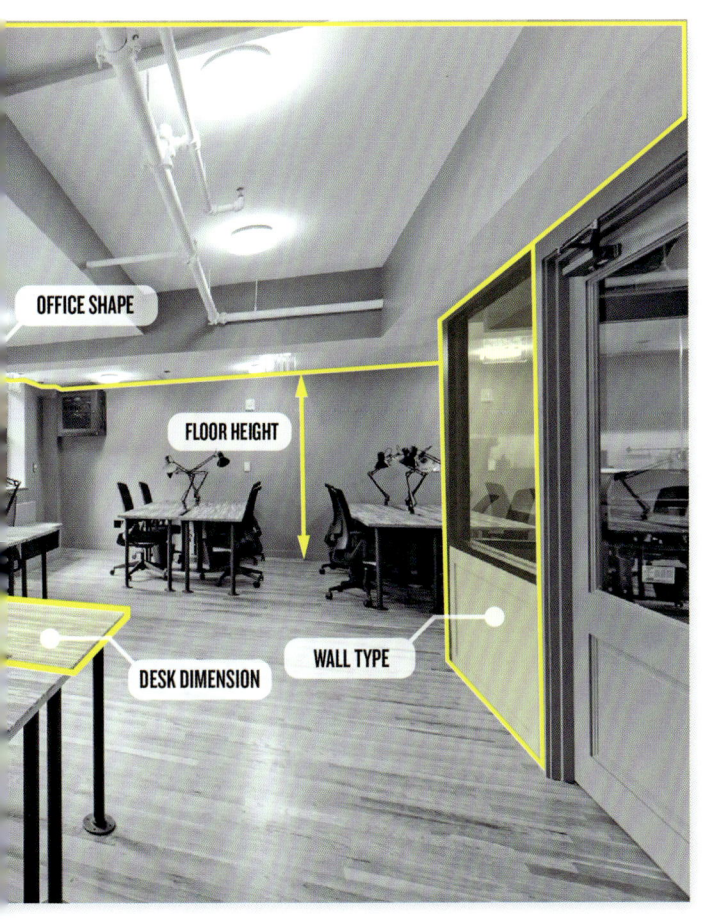

OFFICE SHAPE
FLOOR HEIGHT
DESK DIMENSION
WALL TYPE

Building on Research

In many respects, every architect is a frustrated scientist. They spend years developing hunches about what makes a building successful. They form hypotheses, convince clients to spend millions funding their experiments, and watch their creation rise from the asphalt, crossing their fingers and hoping the building functions as intended. But once the building opens, once it comes time to gather the results from this experiment, architects often find themselves shut out, unable to measure whether their design functioned as intended. The industry being what it is, architects rarely return to their previous work to systematically analyse the consequences of their design choices.

For the most part, the industry's resistance to research is deeply rooted in the institution. It is an institution that rarely measures results, that canonises and celebrates individuals who have shown great intuition, that teaches students to develop and defend design concepts, and that looks to the future while paying little attention to the present. Even if firms were able to conduct research more regularly, most firms do not have the infrastructure to capitalise on the results because they still live and die on their ability to win work instead of the performance of their projects. For this reason, research is not something that can be simply added to practice, but rather something that necessitates rethinking the way we practise altogether. Research needs to be part of the business model, not an accessory added to it. For WeWork, that business model is one of vertical integration, which enables research that incorporates thousands of people, that generalises across projects and that is tied to the financial success of the company. ⌀

WeWork,
Likelihood that people will rent offices at WeWork Moorgate,
London,
2017

Using past sales data, the research team was able to develop a machine-learning model that predicted the likelihood that an individual office will be rented with around 60–70 per cent accuracy.

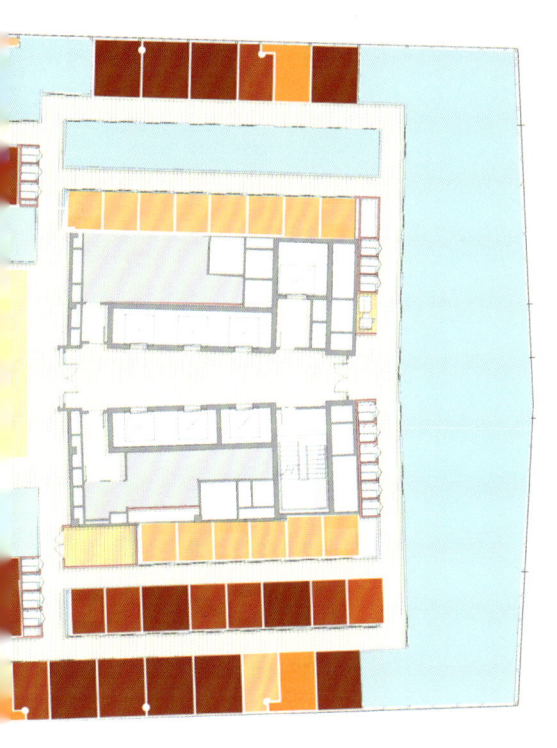

> That business model is one of vertical integration, which enables research that incorporates thousands of people, that generalises across projects and that is tied to the financial success of the company

Notes
1. Frank Duffy, *Work and the City*, Black Dog Publishing (London), 2008, p 12.
2. Leon Festinger *et al*, *Social Pressures in Informal Groups: A Study of Human Factors in Housing*, Harper (Oxford), 1950.
3. Jeanne Arnold *et al*, *Life at Home in the Twenty-First Century: 32 Families Open Their Doors*, Cotsen Institute of Archaeology Press (Los Angeles), 2013.
4. Bill Bordass *et al*, *Probe Strategic Review 1999, Report 4: Strategic Conclusions – Get Real About Building Performance*, The Probe Team (London), 1999; http://www.usablebuildings.co.uk/Probe/ProbePDFs/SR4.pdf.
5. Jane Jacobs, *The Death and Life of Great American Cities*, Random House (New York), 1961.
6. William Whyte, *The Social Life of Small Public Spaces*, documentary film, Project for Public Spaces, 1980.
7. Jan Gehl, *Life Between Buildings: Using Public Space*, Van Nostrand Reinhold (New York), 1971.
8. Festinger, *op cit*.
9. Carlo Bailey *et al*, 'This Room Is Too Dark and the Shape Is Too Long: Quantifying Architectural Design To Predict Successful Spaces', in *Humanising Digital Reality*, Springer (New York), 2017, pp 337–48.
10. Barry LePatner, *Broken Buildings, Busted Budgets: How to Fix America's Trillion-Dollar Construction Industry*, University of Chicago Press (Chicago), 2008.

Text © 2019 John Wiley & Sons Ltd. Images © WeWork

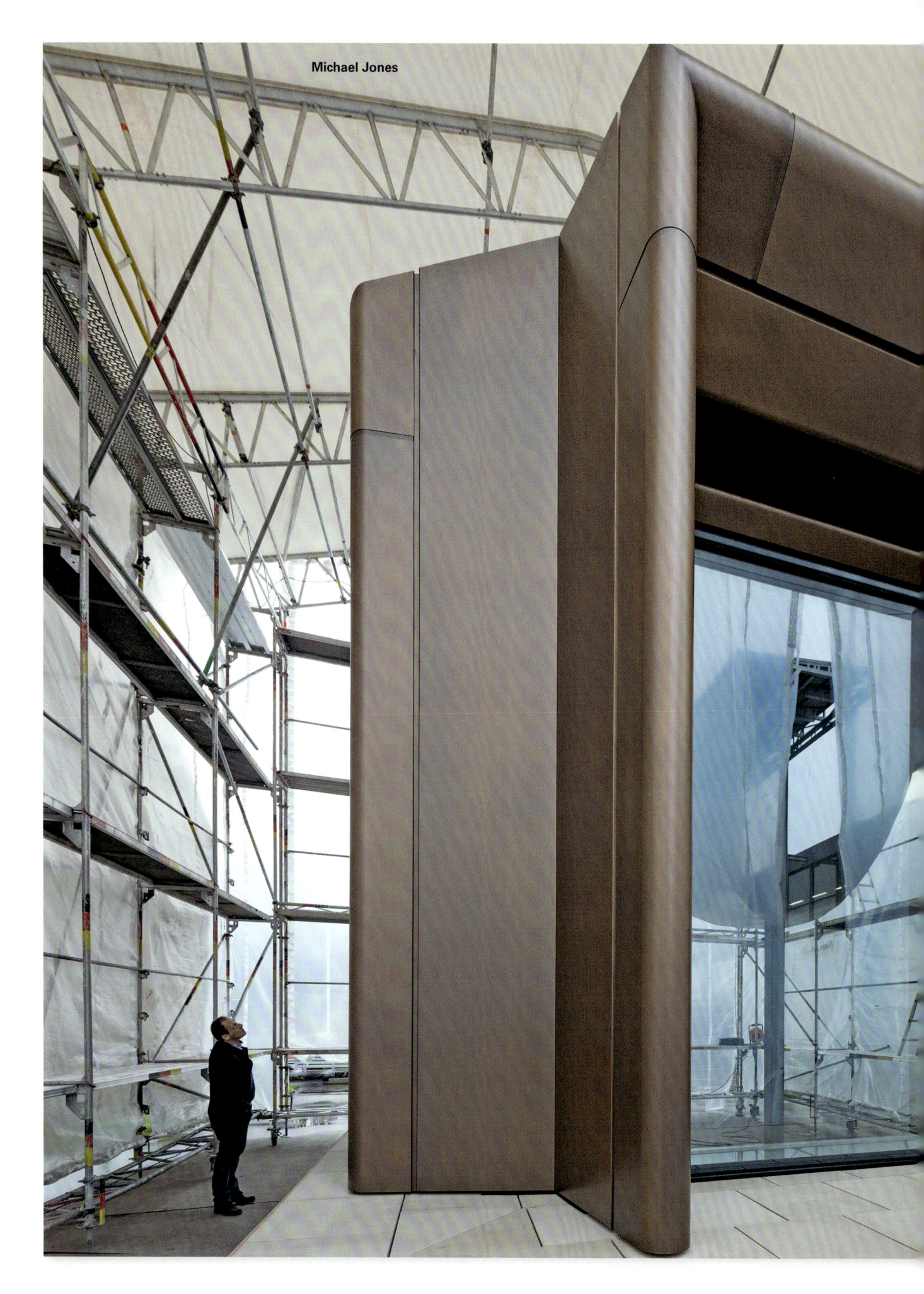

Michael Jones

Pushing the Envelope

Innovation and Collaboration at Bloomberg's New European Headquarters

Foster + Partners' European headquarters building for the global financial information and technology company Bloomberg is exceptional not just for the sheer volume of models and prototypes that were constructed, but also for the level of research that went into it. Several significant elements – notably the innovative breathing facades – were modelled at various scales and in different materials, both physically and virtually, allowing the team to refine them throughout the design process. **Michael Jones**, the project architect, describes how it was done and sets out the added value the method brought to the studio, client and users.

Prototype testing at Gartner factory,
Gundelfingen,
Germany,
2014

Bronze cladding on a facade mock-up being tested at the Gartner factory in Germany.

Bloomberg's new European headquarters is at the heart of the City of London, with a form, massing and materiality which are sensitive to its historic setting yet clearly of its own time. Completed in November 2017, the design and construction of the building was a collaborative enterprise between Bloomberg and Foster + Partners, with unprecedented levels of innovation resulting in a building that is the embodiment of the culture and values of Bloomberg. This article details the scale and depth of research that went into designing the building's natural ventilation system that forms the sustainable focus of the project.

Distinctive Facades

The characteristic facades of the building are a response to not only its historical setting, but also to its sustainable agenda. Large-scale fins made of bronze are set into a deep structural frame in sandstone, which provide solar shading. The fins vary in geometry, density and scale according to aspect, location and exposure to the sun across individual bays of each facade. These also contain openable panels in the rear face of the blade. When outside temperatures permit, these panels open automatically, drawing fresh air directly into the deep plan areas of the building. The internal section of the fin contains an acoustic lining that attenuates the external sounds of the city – a design challenge that has previously largely prohibited the ability to naturally ventilate major buildings in densely populated urban environments. The facade is at the heart of the building's natural ventilation system, whose technical sophistication, elegant detailing and refined materiality reflect the commitment to innovation that underpins the entire project.

Testing and Innovation

Given the extent of innovation on the project, it was important to ensure every aspect of the building was tested, prototyped and mocked-up before it was built. Several parts of the building were modelled at various scales and in different materials, including full-size mock-ups in real materials, allowing the team to refine significant elements throughout the design process. A rigorous research programme was undertaken with a prototype slice of the structure created in a warehouse in Battersea, as well as other working models at the Breathing Buildings test facility in Cambridge and the Gartner factory in Germany.

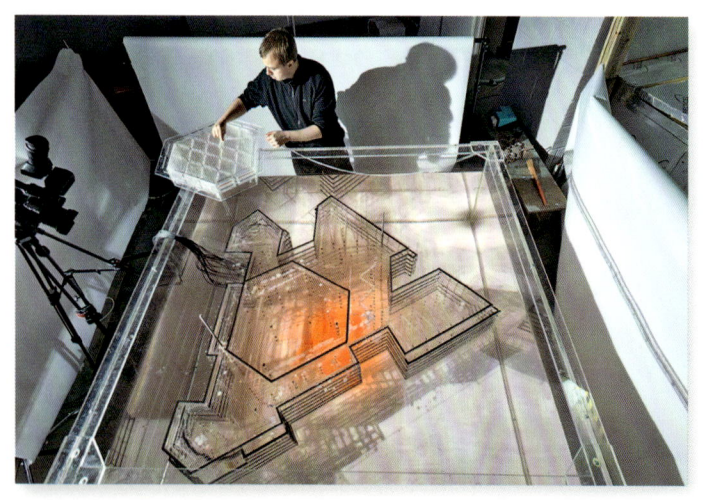

Prototype testing at Breathing Buildings facility, Cambridge, UK, 2013

In 2013, Foster + Partners constructed the world's largest water-bath model in collaboration with Breathing Buildings, to test and validate the movement of air across the Bloomberg building's floor plates.

Foster + Partners,
Bloomberg,
London,
2017

View of Bloomberg from Cannon Street in 2018. In its form, massing and materials, the new building is uniquely of its place and time – a natural extension of the City that will endure and improve the surrounding public realm.

The facade is at the heart of the building's natural ventilation system, whose technical sophistication, elegant detailing and refined materiality reflect the commitment to innovation that underpins the entire project

The building is naturally ventilated, supplemented when necessary by a bespoke chilled ceiling. This was an innovative idea that combined both wellbeing and environmental sustainability, encouraging increased staff productivity, while reducing energy use. It was a challenge for such a deep-plan building because of the large volume of air needed to circulate through it. The predicted air movement was verified through a 1:100 Perspex model immersed in the salt bath, with a dye injected in the water to visualise the system of natural ventilation. This was followed by a full-scale test mock-up, which represented a substantial section of the facade system extending to 25 metres (82 feet) in depth – the distance from facade to atrium. The mock-up comprised a functional version of the facade, including two prototype fins with dual opening inlets and wall panels with temperature control to simulate the glazing. The office space included a heated floor section to simulate solar gain falling onto the floor, together with prototype desk clusters. The heat from people and computers was simulated by calibrated metal tubes and desk-mounted heat mats that produced the appropriate radiant and convective heat flux. The chilled ceiling was installed overhead to be used when required. Additionally, a chamber was constructed outside the facade, allowing air to be introduced at the required temperature to simulate the weather. The last section was a chamber into which the air was drawn from the desk area, functioning as a void.

Foster + Partners team members working in 2015 at the Battersea mock-up site that was commissioned as a test-bed for the environmental and sustainability studies at Bloomberg.

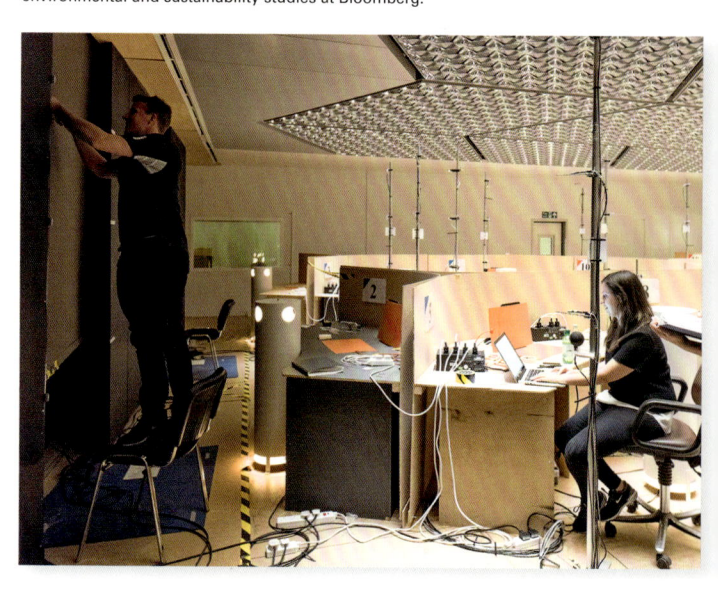

Prototype testing at Bloomberg testing facility, London, 2013-15

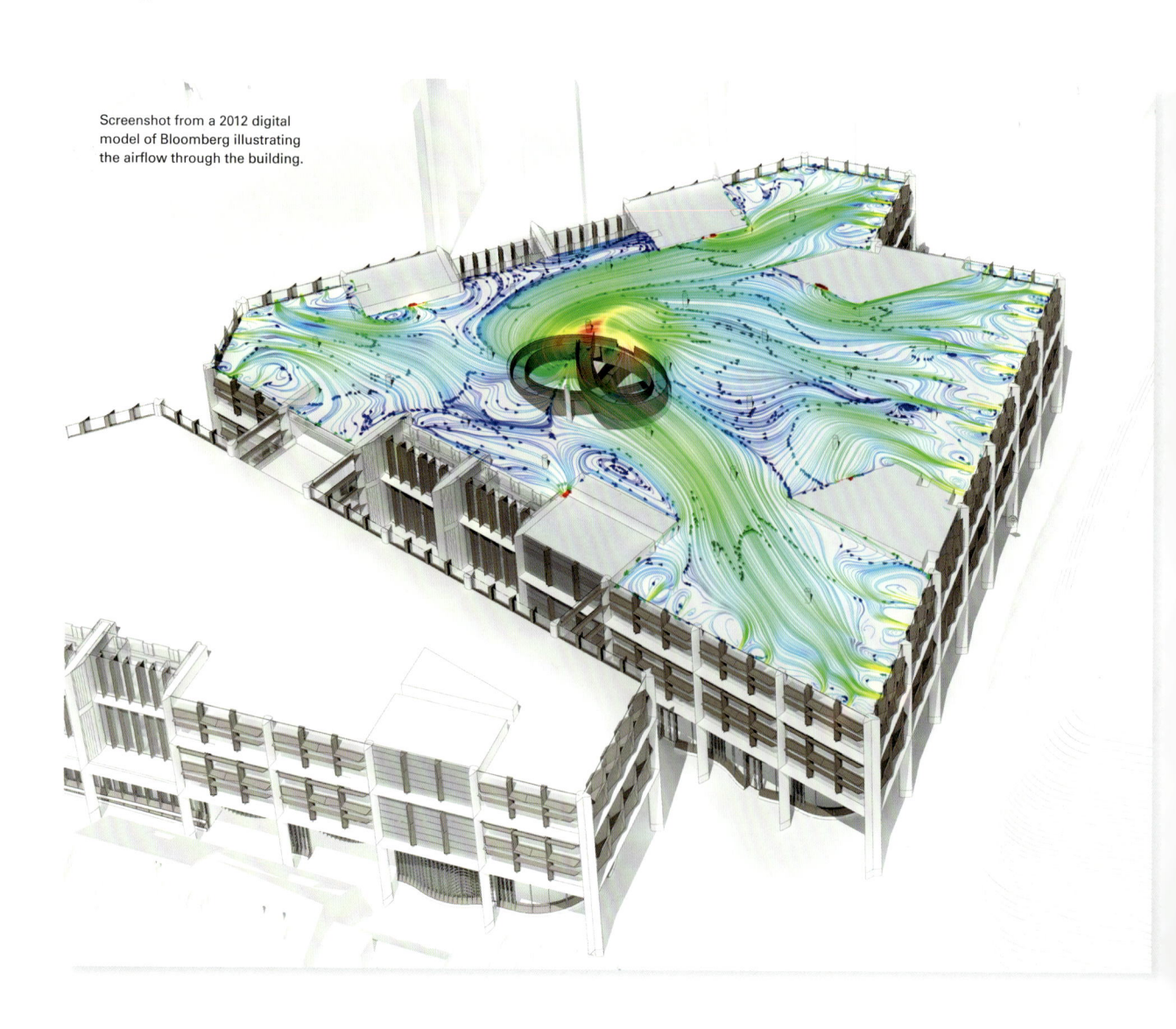

Screenshot from a 2012 digital model of Bloomberg illustrating the airflow through the building.

The mock-up was extensively tested at each desk location, and on mobile sensor trees that allowed investigation of other areas of interest. Air temperature, radiant temperature, relative humidity and air velocity typically at heights representing ankles, seated head, standing head and just below ceiling were all meticulously recorded. The testing was undertaken covering the full range of potential outside air temperatures in increments of 1 degree Celsius (34 degrees Fahrenheit), and at a variety of occupancy densities, represented by varying the heat load in the space. When needed, the chilled ceiling was operated in areas where it would otherwise be uncomfortably warm.

The whole test process took approximately six months. It allowed the team to fine-tune the operating characteristics of the fins, ensuring they could open sufficiently to ventilate the interior spaces, but not such that draughts would occur. The interaction of the chilled ceiling with the occupied space below was also tested, optimising the water temperature to provide a balance between comfort and energy whilst avoiding condensation. The data recorded was then passed to the Building Management System contractor for use in the final building control.

Collaborative Working

Having a client who understood the value of working with industry, as well as the benefits of testing and prototyping, was critical, and Michael Bloomberg was extremely involved throughout the process, visiting the test facility frequently to work with the design team on the many full-size mock-ups, prototypes and testing being progressed there. The process of constant refinement, optimisation and understanding helped reduce risk and ensured that both crucial and subtle changes could be made to the design of the building before construction began. The building has been rated BREEAM Outstanding, with a score of 99.1 per cent – the highest-ever construction-stage score awarded to an office development. This can be attributed in large measure to the innovative design approach and relentless commitment to research and testing, resulting in many solutions that are first-of-their-kind. ᴓ

The design team testing the desk setup in 2014. The notion of teamwork and collaboration flows into the desking systems and layout of each floor.

The individual 'petals' in the ceiling are chilled to cool the occupied floors. They have a large surface area, allowing more efficient cooling than a flat ceiling, thereby reducing the energy consumption of the building.

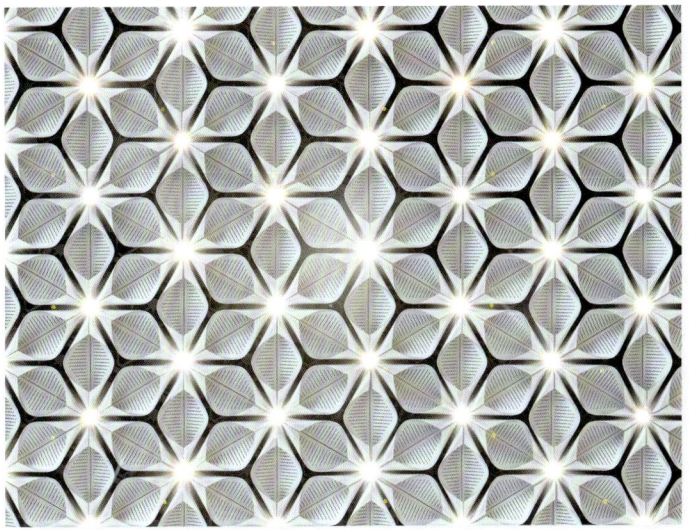

Text © 2019 John Wiley & Sons Ltd. Images © pp 76-9, 80(t), 81 © Nigel Young / Foster + Partners; p 80(b) © Foster + Partners

Rory Hyde

For the Public Good

Rebuilding the Architectural Profession's Social Contract

OMA/AMO, Prada Foundation,
Milan, Italy,
2018

View of the cinema camouflaged by mirrors.

What use is the business of research, when the business of architecture is on its knees? **Rory Hyde** – Curator of Contemporary Architecture and Urbanism at the Victoria and Albert Museum, Adjunct Senior Research Fellow at the University of Melbourne, and Design Advocate for the Mayor of London – argues that architectural research can be a vehicle for escaping architecture's current traps: by asking new kinds of questions, developing new kinds of practice models, and rebuilding the social contract between the profession and the public.

Mies van der Rohe during construction of the Seagram Building, New York, July 1956

According to Matthijs Bouw, the construction of the Seagram Building – completed in 1958 – coincided with a mythical moment that he terms 'peak architecture', when architects held the greatest public respect and the most control over the construction process.

A recent headline in the *Architects' Journal* declared that 'brickies earn more than architects'.[1] Drawing on research from the Federation of Master Builders and the Office of National Statistics, the article showed that not only bricklayers, but practically all those making buildings, including tilers, roofers and carpenters, are paid more than those employed to design them. Of course, there is nothing inherently wrong with this – just because architects sit behind a desk does not make them better – but it does illustrate in stark terms the shocking inability of today's profession to justify its value.

Can research offer a way to escape this fate? How might it be used to re-frame architecture's relationship to clients? Can a new approach to developing knowledge lead to a more persuasive case for the value of the architect? And if so, who stands to benefit from this value? This piece sets out three approaches to design research in practice today, and makes a case for a fourth: one which argues that if the role of the architect is to be valued once again, then architects must deliver broad public good.

Peak Architecture
In contemplating the diminished status of the architect today, it is useful to look back to a time when the tables were turned; a time when the architect commanded great respect, and was valued accordingly. Architect and urbanist Matthijs Bouw describes this mythical moment as 'peak architecture', coinciding with the completion of Mies van der Rohe's Seagram Building in New York in 1958.[2] The Peak Architect held the greatest public respect, the most authorship in the design process, the most control over the construction process, produced the fewest drawings, enjoyed the most freedom from regulation, and made the most money.

The Peak Architect was an artist. They had a singular vision, and it was up to the client to pay for that vision. Any questioning of the vision leads to unacceptable compromise. The Peak Architect got their way by the force of personality, and the apparent inventiveness of their design. It is hard to imagine a time where this could be a viable model for practice, and yet the Peak Architect lives on today in the guise of the 'starchitect', who uses their celebrity status and unusual forms as tools of persuasion.

In research terms, this role is epitomised by AMO – the research studio and think-tank of international practice OMA (see pp 90–95) – who use research to elaborate architecture's capacity as communications and branding. What sets AMO apart is the instrumentality of their advice. They make no claims for the objectivity normally expected of research, offering instead 'singularly targeted advice that is highly biased' for clients including the film company Universal and, most significantly, the fashion brand Prada.[3] Here, research is deployed as a means of persuasion, to justify action rather than evaluate possibilities.

More than a decade on from the great financial crisis of 2008, this model of value looks increasingly fragile. As inequality accelerates, architects who hitch their wagon to the 1 per cent may enjoy a ride to the penthouse, designing rarefied baubles for the super-rich. But this is not a sustainable model for the profession at large, nor does it begin to address the vast challenges facing our cities today.

OMA/AMO,
Prada Foundation,
Milan,
Italy,
2018

OMA and its research arm AMO converted a century-old distillery in Milan into an arts centre for Fondazione Prada. The starchitect is epitomised by AMO/OMA's research studio and think-tank, who use research to elaborate architecture's capacity as communications and branding.

What sets AMO apart is the instrumentality of their advice. They make no claims for the objectivity normally expected of research

Peter Zumthor,
Interior of
Bruder Klaus
Field Chapel,
Mechernich,
Eifel,
Germany,
2007

The project embodies an idea of architecture as material craft, which, as antithesis of starchitecture, prioritises the experience of the senses over the spectacularity of the image.

The realm of material craft spans the seemingly incompatible modes of architecture from the scorched interior of Peter Zumthor's Bruder Klaus Field Chapel in Mechernich, Germany (2007), to the science of the trade literature library

Cover of the paperback edition of Nicholas Negroponte's *The Architecture Machine* (MIT Press, Cambridge, May 1969)

At the dawn of artificial intelligence, Negroponte imagined the computer as a digital 'colleague' and, in so doing, inaugurated the history of the data architect.

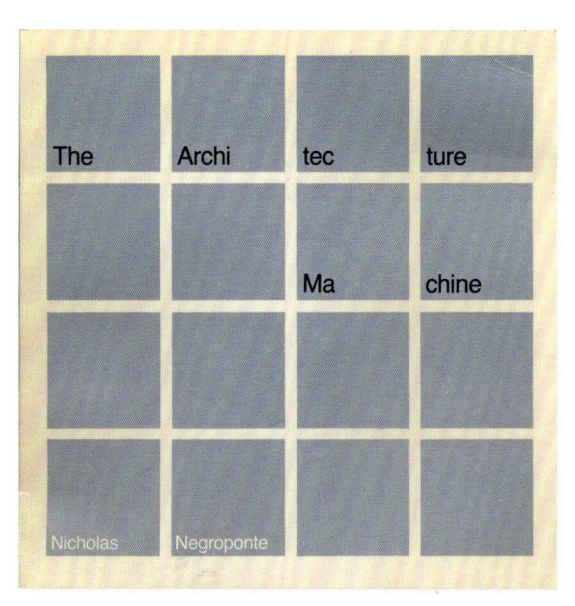

WeWork offices, Chicago, 2016

WeWork are applying big-data analysis to evaluate the design of their office layouts, a process that feeds back into their bottom line.

Material Craft

As such, we can see an emphasis placed on a different kind of value, that of material craft. Presented as the antithesis of starchitecture, the architecture of material craft is justified by its tectonics, the care and intelligence with which physical buildings are assembled, and the gentle power this approach conveys. The 2018 Venice Architecture Biennale was the most substantive showcase for this version of value. It made a claim for an architecture that is humble, grounded in making, and which prioritises the experience of the senses over the spectacularity of the image.

The realm of material craft spans the seemingly incompatible modes of architecture from the scorched interior of Peter Zumthor's Bruder Klaus Field Chapel in Mechernich, Germany (2007), to the science of the trade literature library. Here, architecture is clearly defined by its products – buildings – with no reason to question otherwise.

But does this architecture of material craft cut a path forward, or is it merely a retreat to the past? And how different is it really from starchitecture? Both models make their claim to value in exceptionalism, originality and authorship. These are qualities that depend on their scarcity, and again appeal merely to the 1 per cent. Both starchitecture and the architecture of material craft represent *culs-de-sac* in the future of architecture. Neither offers a viable path forward to an architecture of broad public relevance and social value.

Data

Enter data, the latest claim for architectural value. The data architect is no artist, but a digital scientist, leaning on 'truth' and rationality as justification for their authority. The data architect has a long history, stretching back to Nicholas Negroponte's *The Architecture Machine* of 1969,[4] which, at the dawn of artificial intelligence, imagined the computer as a digital 'colleague', proposing design alternatives and keeping up with a free-flowing conversation. This vision remained out of reach for almost fifty years, but with today's processing power and techniques of data analysis, it finally appears to be a viable model for architecture.

The data architect emerges at the intersection of Silicon Valley tech firms and building information modelling. In the hands of the data architect, architecture is a technocratic process of problem solving. It is of most use in situations that are easily quantified, such as questions of energy efficiency, environmental sustainability or commercial viability. Being close to science, it is most explicitly a form of research, particularly when compared to starchitecture or material craft.

The in-house design team of WeWork, the international network of co-working spaces, is heavily invested in this approach (see pp 68–75). The company has used data derived from their more than 300 office buildings to train a deep-learning algorithm to determine which spaces are most likely to sell, and to specify the optimum size and number of meeting rooms.[5] Similarly, Foster + Partners create elaborate full-scale mock-ups of design proposals, which are subjected to rigorous testing on social and environmental criteria, to ensure the optimum conditions for work – from sound to temperature, moisture and light (see pp 76–81).[6] Both of these prospective data-driven approaches are then evaluated and calibrated with subsequent analysis of the final built projects. This is intensive work, demanding hundreds of hours of effort after the keys have been handed over, and most other architects have moved on to the next job. It is justified by the capturing of data, which has a commercial value. In WeWork's case, this data is valuable because they take on long-term leases and operate the building during occupancy, and therefore the success of their design will return to them in the form of rent. In Foster + Partners' case, this data is valuable because they can demonstrate to their client, and crucially the next client, the empirical efficacy of their design. These are end-to-end systems, where up-front investment in research is directly captured at the completion of the project, and bolsters the company's knowledge base for future work.

Socialising Value
But let us not confuse value to clients with value to society. As long as this data-driven approach is only applied in circumstances of exceptional scale or exceptional budgets, and the value is captured by these exceptional companies, it can only ever be another *cul de sac* of irrelevance. If architecture cannot find a path to broad public utility, we will have failed to learn the lessons of the crash ten years ago, and will not be able to make our way back to a position of broad public value. What does this path look like? And how might research help us to find it?

As we attempt to answer these questions, it is first necessary to look back at the underlying purpose of the professions. Richard and Daniel Susskind in their book *The Future of the Professions* (2015) define the role of professions as 'the way in which expertise is made available in society'.[7] In this broadest sense, a profession is the point of interface between those with specialist knowledge, and the public who are served by the application of this knowledge. This asymmetrical relationship is enabled by what they term a 'grand bargain', a social contract that grants exclusivity over a domain of knowledge in exchange for applying this knowledge for the benefit of all.

Foster + Partners,
South Beach Development,
Singapore,
2016

Render diagram of the parametric performance-driven canopy project. This project for an urban quarter combines new construction with the restoration of existing buildings. A wide landscaped pedestrian avenue weaves through the site, connecting the primary circulation routes and public spaces and protecting them via a large canopy of steel and aluminium louvres. The canopy was designed in the light of Specialist Modelling Group environmental research and analysis of the temperature and humidity levels of an unshaded walkway.

This approach would apply the full potential of emerging technologies not just for the narrowly defined benefit of our explicit clients, but would also meet our professional obligations to society at large

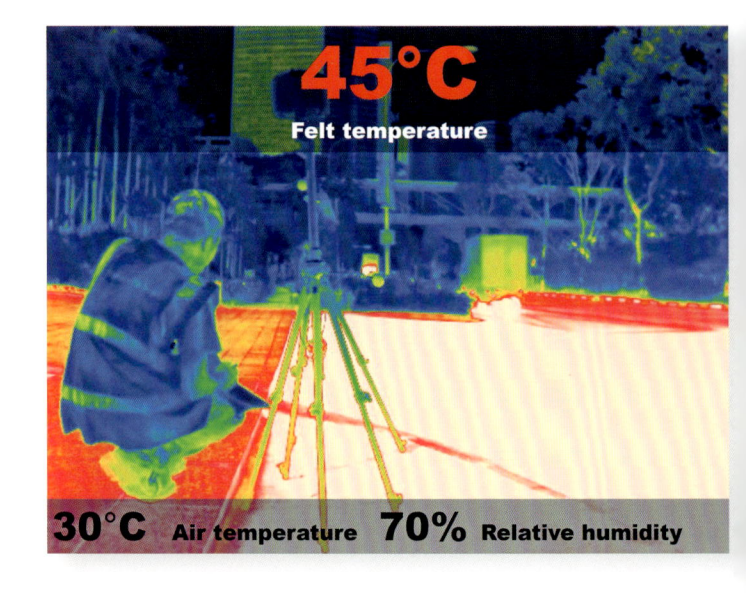

Text © 2019 John Wiley & Sons Ltd. Images: pp 82-3, Photograph by Iwan Baan, Courtesy of OMA; p 84 Photo by Frank Scherschel/The LIFE Picture Collection/Getty Images; p 85 Photograph by Bas Princen, Courtesy of Fondazione Prada; p 86 Photo by Lothar M. Peter/ullstein bild via Getty Images; p 87(t) © 1970 Massachusetts Institute of Technology. Reproduced courtesy of The MIT Press; p 87(b) Photo by Interim Archives/Getty Images; pp 88-9(t), 88(b) © Foster + Partners; p 89(b) © Nigel Young/Foster + Partners

In the case of architecture, architects are responsible for maintaining and applying this body of specialist knowledge on behalf of society at large in exchange for an exclusive and protected right to this work. But are architects holding up their end of the bargain? Architects are responsible for a vanishingly small amount of the built environment, neglecting the reality of where the vast majority of people live, or the daily challenges they face.

For an alternative model of professional knowledge management, we ought to look to medicine as an example. The social democratic triumph of the UK's National Health Service is above all a triumph of knowledge management and application. When health is understood to be a public right, the provision of this service is organised in such a way as to serve all in society. Research is undertaken by universities, hospitals and specialists, who publish their findings and ensure the discipline as a whole moves forward together. General Practitioners operate in the front lines, applying this knowledge, and collating data on the effectiveness at the patient level. Together, these various interrelated components work to effectively serve society as a whole.

If we were to consider architecture a public right – to safe streets, decent housing, classrooms that encourage attention, public buildings that inspire trust in institutions, and so on – then how might we reorganise the research, management and application of architectural knowledge to serve these aims?

This is where a democratised version of the data-driven approach could help. If we were to reconceive of the architectural project as an obligation to the entire city, rather than our own portfolios, then we could begin to reimagine architectural practice as an open, collaborative, cooperative endeavour. The research generated by individual practices, which currently lives on individual servers, could be shared and cross-referenced, creating a giant knowledge base which all practitioners could draw from. Tools of big data could be used to trawl this pool of information to extract archetypal responses to common questions, ranging from how to do a house extension to how to plan a neighbourhood. The criteria for evaluating these archetypes would be aligned with the public good. And the sharing of knowledge would help us meet the scale of the challenge, rather than the extreme waste in duplication that plagues current professional knowledge sharing. This approach would apply the full potential of emerging technologies not just for the narrowly defined benefit of our explicit clients, but would also meet our professional obligations to society at large.

If we hope to be paid more than brickies, this is the very least we should set out to achieve. 𝔻

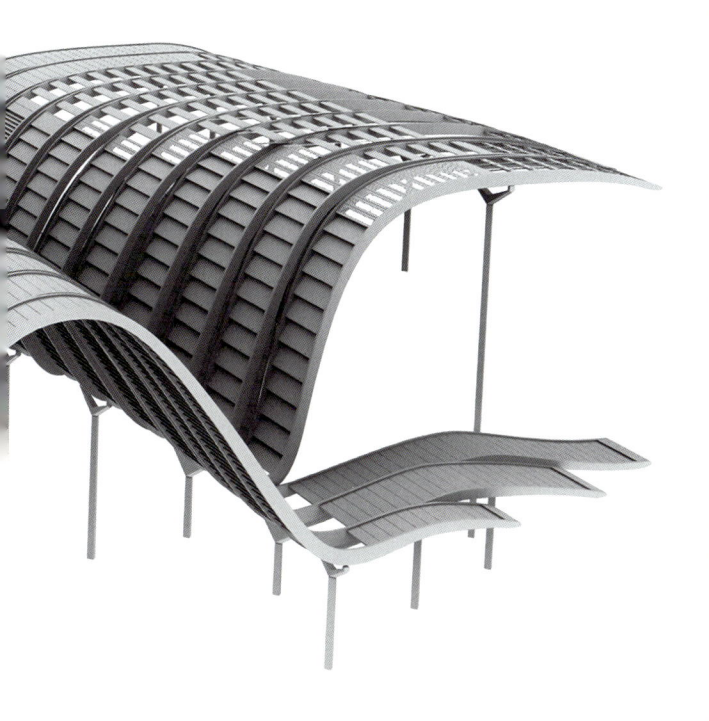

Foster + Partners, South Beach Development, Singapore, 2016

above: 1:1 mock-up of the canopy, testing the angle of the louvres to encourage natural ventilation.

opposite: This project for an urban quarter combines new construction with the restoration of existing buildings. A wide landscaped pedestrian avenue weaves through the site, connecting the primary circulation routes and public spaces and protecting them via a large canopy of steel and aluminium louvres. The canopy was designed in the light of Specialist Modelling Group environmental research and analysis of the temperature and humidity levels of an unshaded walkway.

Notes
1. Greg Pitcher, 'Brickies "Earn More Than Architects"', *Architects' Journal*, 6 March 2018; www.architectsjournal.co.uk/news/brickies-earn-more-than-architects/10028791.article.
2. Interview by Rory Hyde with Matthijs Bouw, February 2017.
3. Michael Speaks, 'Design Intelligence, Part 3: AMO', interview with Jeffrey Inaba, *A+U: Architecture and Urbanism*, 389 (2), 2003, pp 130–37.
4. Nicholas Negroponte, *The Architecture Machine*, MIT Press (Cambridge, MA), 1969; first published in hardback in 1970 as *The Architecture Machine: Toward a More Human Environment*.
5. Presentation from Daniel Davis, WeWork Director of Research, Business of Research symposium, London, 3 July 2018.
6. Presentation from Irene Gallou, Partner of Foster + Partners, Business of Research symposium, London, 3 July 2018.
7. Richard Susskind and Daniel Susskind, *The Future of the Professions: How Technology will Transform the Work of Human Experts*, Oxford University Press (Oxford), 2015, p 9.

OMA,
De Rotterdam,
Rotterdam,
Netherlands,
2013

Programme section. Conceived as a vertical city, the project comprises three interconnected mixed-use towers that provide both clarity and synergy for residents and office workers alike.

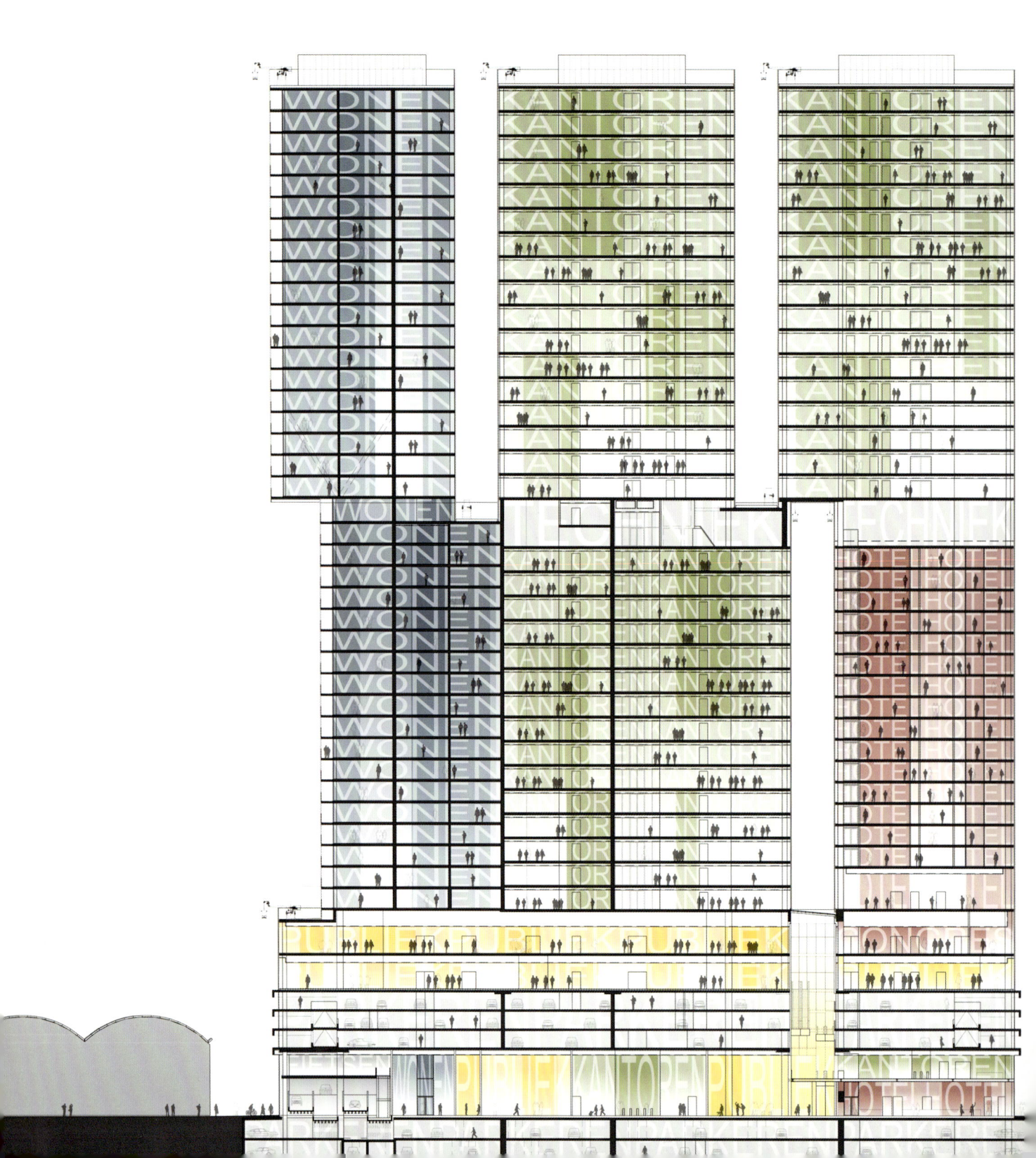

The Germination of Preoccupations
Research Infiltration

From its foundation as the Office for Metropolitan Architecture in Rotterdam, Netherlands, OMA has expanded to have bases on four continents. What binds the practice together is a relentlessly intellectual approach that informs not only its buildings, but also its work in academia, publishing and exhibitions through its research and design studio AMO. **Carol Patterson**, a director for OMA in London, gives the lowdown on how it evolved and how some projects can serve as a research basis for others.

OMA offices,
Rotterdam,
Netherlands,
2018

Snapshot of a corner of OMA at work, illustrating the variety of media adjacent to a team.

'Research' is a word often used by architectural firms to indicate an exercise undertaken early in a project. Watch a PowerPoint presentation by an architect in the initial stages of design, or during a pitch, and you will see a slide, if not a full section, titled 'Research', 'Context', 'History', 'References' or a favourite Briticism: 'Opportunities and Constraints' – as if to reassure that what comes after is the result of a rational process of analysis. Why can it not just be accepted that site and legislative issues are constraints, and working strategically amongst them is what drives exceptional design?

At the Office for Metropolitan Architecture (OMA), 'research' is not so much a workstream to rationalise or inspire, but rather the intellectual interrogation of given parameters. Relentless examination of the issues, whether they be constraints, opportunities or aberrations is in OMA's DNA. This research permeates the output of the office across different media, from architectural design to publication, exhibition, academia and built form.

OMA,
Universal Headquarters,
Los Angeles,
California,
1996

Specific departments are expressed in vertical towers, generic office space in the horizontal, and all speared together mid-air by a 'corporate beam'.

Preoccupations

Building types and eras, programme, use and place infiltrate OMA's output. What may start as an examination of type – library, shopping, performance or the workplace – perhaps during a competition, reappears in lectures and publications, expanding and readapting through realised work.

Take, for example, the seemingly mundane topic 'workplace'. In 1996, OMA was commissioned by the film studio Universal to design their headquarters in Los Angeles. While the project is unbuilt, the examination (call it 'research') of how a media company functions, and how the formal proposal for the departmental relationships – specific departments in vertical towers, while generic office space is in the horizontal, speared together mid-air by a 'corporate beam' – could foster creativity, became the set piece for future investigations.

Mind the Book

The project for Universal was published in *a+u* as 'OMAa+uNiversal, 100% Design Development: Universal Building'.[1] Publishing has been an integral part of OMA's output since the beginning. OMA co-founder Rem Koolhaas published *Delirious New York* in 1978,[2] concurrent with the time the office was established. Seventeen years later, *S,M,L,XL*[3] preceded the expanding portfolio of built work at the turn of the century.

Similarly, the office has a tentacled relationship to academia. Atypically, rather than the principals maintaining a design studio at a neighbouring institution, OMA staff – from partners to interns – are involved across academia internationally. Through running design studios, lecturing, and establishing new institutions such as the Strelka Institute for Media, Architecture and Design in Moscow, never mind the diaspora of former staff populating universities around the globe, the investigative nature of academia infiltrates. The preoccupations of the office pass out into academia, and circle back.

Publishing has been an integral part of OMA's output since the beginning

OMA,
Balcony book stack,
Rotterdam,
Netherlands,
2018

A small selection of OMA publications. Though none are specific to buildings, the studies in some led to future commissions.

OMA,
Rijnstraat 8,
The Hague,
Netherlands,
2017

Bringing the outside in, literally, while extending the notion of open working.

AMO(ment) in time
These strands converged around the time of Universal, in the late 1990s, when the staff was burgeoning. Research under the *Harvard Design School Guide to Shopping* (2001)[4] gave the office expertise in a domain that went beyond the materiality of buildings, and the fashion house Prada selected OMA to collaborate on their expanding brand with flagship buildings in three US cities. It was at this time that AMO was established, setting apart the non-building work of the office from the standard practice of an architectural enterprise.

OMA,
Axel Springer Campus,
Berlin,
due for completion 2020

The open workplace in contrast to the traditional, culminating in a valley of terraces.

Back to Work(place)

De Rotterdam is a project in The Hague that began in 1997 – on the heels of Universal – and was put on hold, restarted, held, restarted, until the markets aligned for it to be built. Conceived as a vertical city, by the time De Rotterdam was completed in 2013, so had been a London office headquarters for the Rothschild bank (2011), and competitions won for Rijnstraat 8 in The Hague (completed 2017) and for the Axel Springer Campus in Berlin (due for completion early 2020). Concepts tested at Universal – ie generic horizontality and vertical specificity – were reapplied against differing briefs and organisations in the ensuing projects. Generic office floors at the main cube of Rothschild contrast with the base and top of the building where special spaces are created, finished in modern reinterpretations of the history of the company. At De Rotterdam, the programmatic difference from the generic office is expressed in the overall form of the building, with varying tower facades and a horizontal raised car park slicing across the base. Rijnstraat 8 combines two ministries and two governmental organisations into a single refurbished 1980s building, opening atriums for use and changing the nature of open working. At Axel Springer the traditional enclosed workspace is counterposed against open terraced floors which are further exposed to form a digital valley.

While a specific 'workplace' project does not exist, the research undertaken in 1996–7 for Universal and De Rotterdam has been a seed for germinating on the topic, which has passed through a generation of project teams and been utilised in lectures, included in design proposals (at times rejected), and recirculated again to be realised in recent work. This preoccupation may or may not be brought back into academia by a current or future collaborator, and may or may not become a publication. One does not necessarily follow the other; it is a self-generating infiltration. 𐤀

At Axel Springer the traditional enclosed workspace is counterposed against open terraced floors

Notes
1. *OMAa+uNiversal, 100% Design Development: Universal Building, Architecture & Urbanism (a+u)* special issue, 364, May 2001.
2. Rem Koolhaas, *Delirious New York: A Retroactive Manifesto for Manhattan*, Oxford University Press (New York), 1978.
3. OMA, Rem Koolhaas, Bruce Mau, *S,M,L,XL*, The Monacelli Press (New York), 1995.
4. Chuihua Judy Chung, Jeffrey Inaba, Rem Koolhaas and Sze Tsung Leong, *Project on the City 2: Harvard Design School Guide to Shopping*, Taschen (Cologne and New York), 2001.

Text © 2019 John Wiley & Sons Ltd. Images: pp 90-1, 92(t), 93 © OMA; p 92(b) © OMA, photo by Hans Werlemann; p 94 © Nick Guttrige, courtesy of OMA; p 95 Photograph by Frans Parthesius, Courtesy of OMA

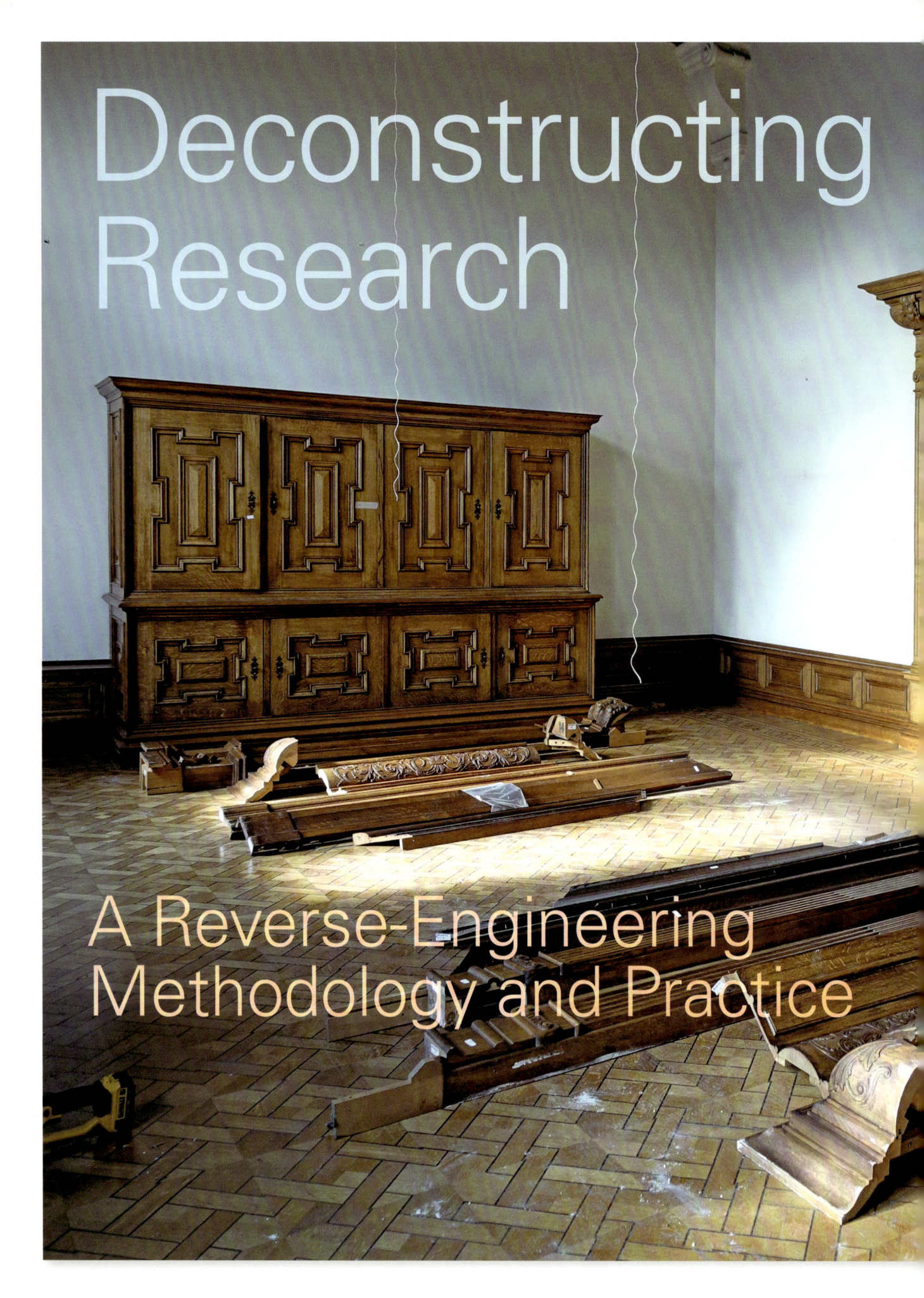

Deconstructing Research

A Reverse-Engineering Methodology and Practice

Alison Creba and Lionel Devlieger

Brussels architecture and art collective Rotor's approach involves research through physical immersion in each project site. By engaging with people's lived realities and reinvesting knowledge in the places where it was acquired, they have gained particular prominence in the flourishing reuse sector. Rotor's resident researcher **Alison Creba** and co-founder **Lionel Devlieger** here describe how they work, and present some of their projects, in Belgium and Sicily.

```
Rotor DC,
Antwerp City Hall interior deconstruction,
Antwerp,
Belgium,
2017
```

Without heritage designation, these architectural features would have otherwise gone to landfill. Instead, Rotor demounted and salvaged them.

Formed in 2005 by a handful of young professionals interested in the material environment and the building industry, Belgium-based architecture and art collective Rotor has grown into a finely coordinated group of around 20 people with complementary backgrounds in architecture, engineering, scenography and production. Motivated to transform not only spaces and materials, but also the values associated with them, the collective's practice has developed through a dynamic interdisciplinary research framework and methodology involving hands-on experience, formal historical and technical investigations and experimental fieldwork that has resulted in projects ranging from the deconstruction and salvage of a city hall interior in Antwerp, Belgium as part of a larger restoration initiative, to interventions in abandoned concrete structures on a hillside near Palermo in Italy, and a series of accessible policy-level publications.

While early projects identified value in unoccupied industrial land and overlooked building materials, they also helped to develop Rotor's reputation as a critical voice within sustainable architecture discourse. Focusing on materials reuse as the most efficient way to address the massive volumes of waste generated through construction, renovation and demolition (CRD) processes, its scope has since expanded to include public and private consultancy work for tenders in building deconstruction and architectural salvage. In 2014, it launched Rotor DC, a for-profit sister company organised as a cooperative, which facilitates the deconstruction and sale of materials directly from the work site, via an online store or in its spacious showroom in Brussels.

Complementing the resourceful premise of its early projects, the practice's expertise in materials reuse developed through research commissions conducted on behalf of various regional public administrations. Indeed, following the 2008 publication of the *EU Waste Framework Directive* which established ambitious targets for the reduction of CRD waste by 2020,[1] Rotor's research services were sought to conduct an analysis of building and demolition waste in Brussels and an overview of the Belgian reuse sector, work that supplemented the limited capacities of the city's relatively small public administration and provided the practice with insight into untapped business opportunities. As consultants, entrepreneurs and researchers, Rotor's cyclical method of working – investigating, testing and applying knowledge of the field – has led to it becoming a successful practice in the burgeoning reuse sector.

An understanding of the symbolic power of objects to communicate nuanced ideas has also allowed the collective's practice to evolve through involvement in the design and execution of exhibitions for the Venice Architecture Biennale (2010), Prada (2011) and OMA (2012), among others. In projects such as these, abstract expression is also an opportunity for research. Exploring topics such as borderlessness, invasive species and the legacy of human intervention in the landscape, Rotor's artistic endeavours have also enabled a broader analysis of the conditions that affect materials reuse.

While diverse in nature, all Rotor's projects are informed by a consistent methodology rooted in a respect for the lived conditions of the topics the collective explores. In considering the experiences of workers on site as well as the relationships between contractors and materials suppliers, Rotor's research extends beyond books and into the real world. Conceptually very simple, this approach involves physical immersion in a site through observation of and interaction with its users. Three projects in particular especially demonstrate the varied results of this immersive process of documentation, collection and representation – of deconstructing research.

Removing and Preserving Building Elements

In the summer of 2017, a team from Rotor DC spent three weeks partially deconstructing interior portions of the Stadhuis – Antwerp's historic City Hall – in anticipation of a large renovation project. A rare example of the Flemish Renaissance style of the 1560s, the building is inscribed on UNESCO's World Heritage List. Understanding not only the symbolic cultural value of the whole structure, but also the economic and environmental benefits of recovering these interior elements, the City of Antwerp awarded Rotor the deconstruction contract. The team was tasked with the removal of features that had been installed following successive fires in the 19th and 20th centuries that did not meet contemporary fire standards or conflicted with the restoration initiatives at hand.

After conducting a detailed inventory and evaluation of materials with high reuse values, the team carefully documented and disassembled a range of components: from parquet and limestone flooring to wall sconces and decorative mirrors. For Rotor, however, the process of deconstruction is always also a research project. At the Stadhuis, demounting seemingly cohesive elements unveiled complex assemblies and structural nuances. The process also revealed new bureaucratic dimensions: whereas tenders for deconstruction were frequent up until the 19th century, this project was the first of its kind for the city of Antwerp in almost a hundred years. It also engendered an elaborate joint communication campaign to publicise the process and products. Indeed, the items salvaged proved their worth; their high cultural value meant they were quickly sold within the first month. In turn, the funds generated through the sale of the materials were fed back into the cooperative, reimbursing the costs of labour, transportation, restoration and temporary storage. Ultimately confirming the viability of Rotor DC's business model, the project also reinforced the social values associated with its deconstruction initiatives and highlighted a strong interest among the local community for retaining and integrating salvaged materials.

> The project also reinforced the social values associated with its deconstruction initiatives and highlighted a strong interest among the local community for retaining and integrating salvaged materials

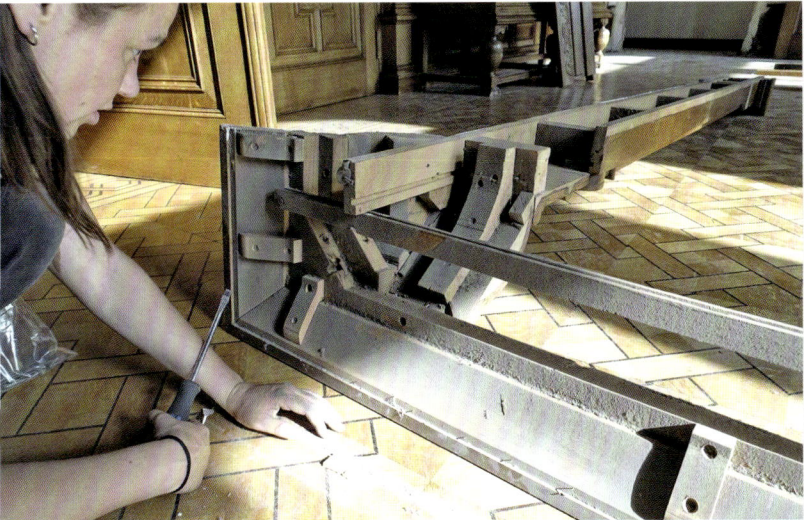

Rotor DC,
Antwerp City Hall interior deconstruction,
Antwerp,
Belgium,
2017

above: When listed for sale on Rotor DC's online inventory (rotordc.com), assemblages are shown in their integrity, as they appeared before dismantling.

left: Rotor's deconstruction practice is a form of research – where the physical act of taking-apart supplements the knowledge of the individual components harvested from the site.

Mapping the Distance From Here to Utopia

Rotor's 2017 book *Déconstruction et réemploi: Comment faire circuler les éléments de construction* (*Deconstruction and Reuse: How to Get Building Materials to Circulate*)[2] recapitulates research developed in collaboration with the Belgian Building Research Institute with funding from the European Regional Development Fund (ERDF) and the Brussels-Capital Region. Expanding on earlier research commissions for the latter, it positions architectural materials reuse within a historical context as well as within a contemporary discourse on the circular economy. As such, it was not part of the contractual deliverables for the project, which included a legal report on certification markings for reused components and an 'inspirational document' intended for public building experts and policy makers, but instead an extension of the latter report that was eventually upgraded to a book with a far wider target audience.

Now in its second print, the publication is an investigation of the existing conditions, historical precedents and practical frameworks for the identification and reintegration of reused construction materials. It gives a hopeful but frank account, detailing also the many hurdles that stand in the way of scaling up reuse practices. The wide-ranging nature of these challenges (economic, technical, logistical, legal, aesthetic) also gives a taste of Rotor's eclectic research interests. Because the public funding for the project stipulated that the output be publicly accessible, Rotor hosted a public tender process to select a publisher for the book. In addition to organising the printing and distribution, Rotor also arranged for copies of the book to be made freely available in university and public libraries throughout Belgium.

Rotor,
Cover of *Déconstruction et réemploi*,
2017

Written by Rotor, the book is an inspirational document that provides both historical and contemporary investigations of demolition, deconstruction and materials reuse in Belgium.

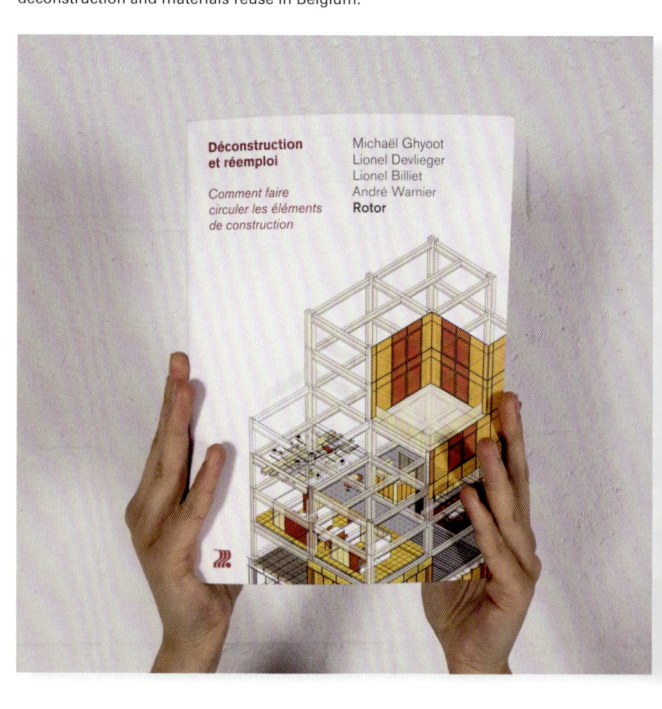

Portrait of a demolisher at work,
c 1900

The Archives of the City of Brussels hold this historical portrait of a wrecker on a demolition site, revealing that deconstruction practices were common before the turn of the century.

Architectural salvage yard,
Kampenhout,
Belgium,
2016

Cleaned salvaged bricks, ready for reuse. The image is from one of hundreds of site visits Rotor made to architectural salvage yards across Belgium, research that resulted in the development of the practice's Opalis.be online inventory that not only connects salvaged material suppliers with eager consumers, but also reinforces the existence of the broader reuse sector.

Rotor,
From Up Here, It's a Whole Other Story,
Pizzo Sella,
Palermo,
Italy,
2018

As a part of its project for the Manifesta 12 nomadic European art biennale, Rotor intervened in the striking landscape of Pizzo Sella, known as the 'hill of shame', where the incomplete concrete structures have come to represent corruption, rapid development and environmental destruction.

Rotor led hikes along a rugged path historically used by herders and local wildlife. A form of research in and of itself, these expeditions constitute both method and practice. A meditative process, the journeys also allowed participants to gain new perspectives of this controversial landscape.

As both the subject and the frame, part of Rotor's contribution to Manifesta 12 involved architectural interventions into a single structure aimed at offering visitors a nuanced view of the surrounding landscape.

Addressing the Physicality of the 'Hill of Shame'

Rotor's immersive research approach is also visible in its artistic endeavours, such as its project for Manifesta 12 – a nomadic European art biennale which in 2018 took place on multiple sites in and around Palermo in Italy. For the five-month exhibition, Rotor was invited by curators to intervene on Pizzo Sella, a promontory famous for its a surreal landscape of 170 abandoned concrete structures that represent a point of contestation for the city at large. The result of a series of dubious building permits awarded in the late 1980s, these incomplete forms permanently altered the hillside, which had previously been designated a nature conservation area. The more than 30 years since have been marked both by propositions to demolish the remaining structures, as well as negotiations allowing a small group of property owners to reside on the hill.

Understanding the many complex associations with the site, Rotor's project entitled From Up Here, It's a Whole Other Story aimed not to resolve, but to reveal the nuances of this local issue by inviting the public to visit the hill, its structures and the surrounding landscape. Engaging not just with the politically charged structures, but also with the plant and animal life, its histories and views, Rotor's broad examination of the hillside revealed a historical path containing traces of past dwellings, brick ovens and local wildlife. As a manifestation of these physical and bureaucratic investigations, the team used materials harvested from nearby ruins to make both the structures and pathway safe and hospitable for visitors in order to invite a new way of not only looking at the existing setting, but also considering broader questions on the future and conservation of the landscape. Beyond this, the project was largely shaped by volunteers who responded to Rotor's open call for a series of workshops in the lead up to the opening event. In this way, the project was conceived not only as a means for researching and expressing ideas on a landscape-scale, but also as a generative pedagogical experience.

Circling Back

While varied, the work described here demonstrates Rotor's approach to engaging with the lived realities of a project through direct involvement with its subject. Building on observations, materials and experiences gathered on site, the collective's work takes its cues from both historical references and empirical data to inform future pursuits. Finally, and perhaps most importantly, Rotor's projects are unified in their practice of reinvesting knowledge in the communities from which it was extracted. Here, proprietors of salvage yards, building owners, contractors, architects, public officials, academics and local residents are simultaneously reintroduced and empowered to forge new relationships within their unique contexts. In this sense, the architecture of reuse poetically permeates Rotor's research practice and enforces a more sensitive attention to its broader environmental context. ᴆ

Note
1. European Commission, 'Directive 2008/98/EC on Waste (Waste Framework Directive)'; http://ec.europa.eu/environment/waste/framework/.
2. Michaël Ghyoot, Lionel Devlieger, Lionel Billet and André Warnier, *Déconstruction et réemploi: Comment faire circuler les éléments de construction*, Presses Polytechniques et Universitaires Romandes (Lausanne), 2017.

Text © 2019 John Wiley & Sons Ltd. Images: pp 96–9, 100(t&b) © Rotor; p 100(c) © Archives de la Ville de Bruxelles, AVB C-14571, photo: J.Geuens/Berlarij; p 101 © Photos Alison Creba, 2018

Jane Hall

Building Practices

The Infrastructure of Materials Research

Materials testing is fundamental to multidisciplinary collective Assemble's practice. Trialling large-scale prototypes in the South London workshop space which they share with various other craft makers and artists allows further cross-disciplinary pollination of ideas through mutual observation. Assemble member **Jane Hall** sets out how they achieve innovation at low cost through mixing standard components with bespoke elements. Their recent project for the facade cladding of the nearby Goldsmiths Centre for Contemporary Art serves as an example.

Assemble,
Goldsmiths Centre
for Contemporary Art,
New Cross,
London,
2018

Assemble tested a number of different acid stains on fibre-cement board as part of the facade development.

Assemble's practice is predicated on the ability to make things themselves as a means to experience the tactility of materials during the process of design. As a collective of 20 people who work collaboratively, the first projects were largely designed on site during the process of construction, and as such the studio remains organised cooperatively and without hierarchy. This dynamic is sustained through the use of large-scale 1:1 prototypes as a means to communicate within the group, but also to enable a more accessible approach to design that allows for a collective sense of authorship of the work. While this has allowed the blurring of boundaries between the role of designer, contractor, builder and, on occasion, occupier, it also runs inherent risks. As Assemble has grown and the projects increasingly intersect with traditional channels of procurement, its materials research has therefore evolved within the practice as a means to adapt a methodology of group thinking to the constraints of more conventional forms of delivery, where projects are less likely to be self-built. Indicative of this shift in the collective's design process is the Goldsmiths Centre for Contemporary Art (CCA) gallery space in London (2018), which explores materials within the construction of its facade.

Assemble,
Goldsmiths Centre for
Contemporary Art,
New Cross,
London,
2018

The gallery space is housed within a Grade II-listed Victorian bath house.

Vertical articulation was achieved using a standard roofing ridge piece, a cornice detail through the repurposing of an apron flashing piece, and cills from cutting and shaping a coping piece

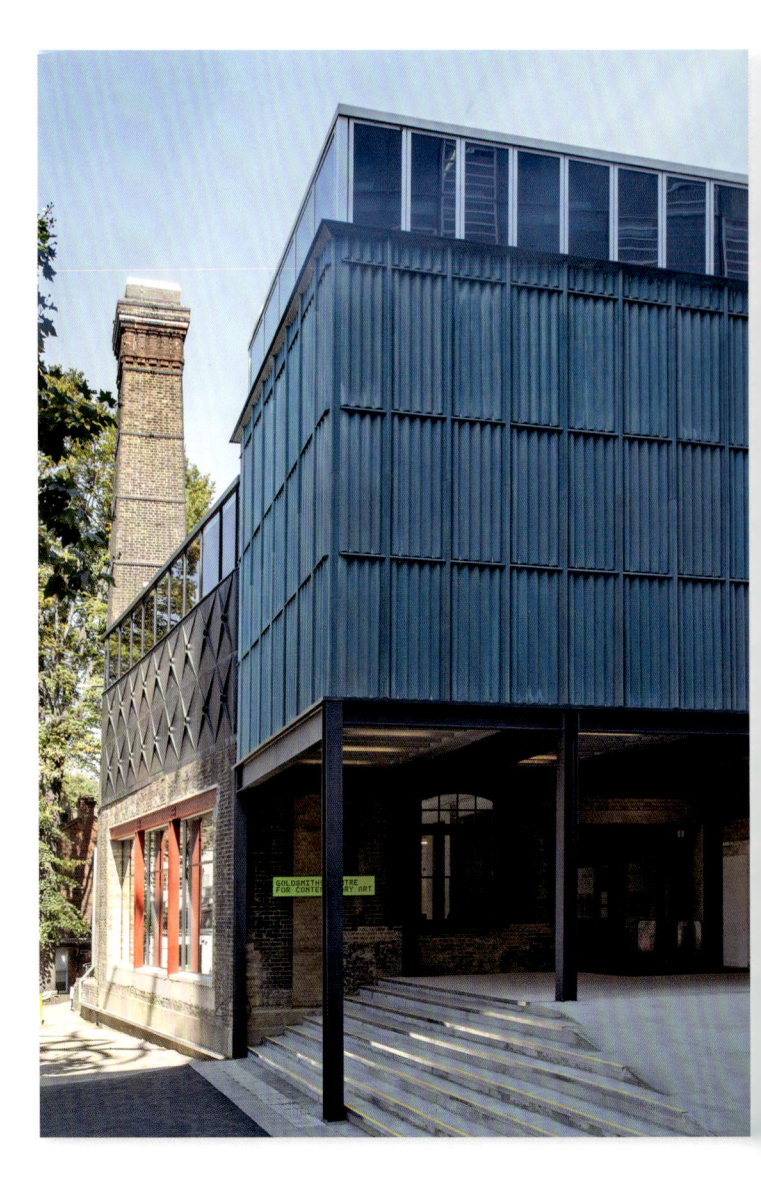

The new art centre at the heart of the Goldsmiths, University of London campus in New Cross explores materials within the construction of its facade.

above: A fragment of the facade for the new centre was built at 1:1 in Assemble's studio in order to test the detailing of the final design.

below: The collective works with a number of large-scale models during its design process. For the Goldsmiths competition, a 1:20 sectional model showed the range of both existing and proposed gallery spaces.

Won through an open competition in 2014, the commission for Goldsmiths, University of London was a departure from the self-constructed projects upon which Assemble's practice model previously relied. While the collective continued to develop the design with the client through the use of large-scale models, it evolved with little hands-on involvement from the wider group, who were only able to work within representational scales rather than at 1:1 due to the requirement to deliver the project within the framework of set RIBA stages, which became a cause of increasing frustration. However, working within the restrictions of a Grade II listed building and the continued constraints on cost resulted unexpectedly in the opportunity to experiment with the new-build elements of the project, achieving innovations in materiality born from the limitations of the budget. The cladding system, for example, was built as a 1:1 mock-up in Sugarhouse Studios, a former school building in Bermondsey, South London where Assemble shares a workshop space with a number of carpenters, ceramicists, designers, artists and other makers. The large-scale working model was used to refine the design for the new parts of the building's facade, with various acid stains tested on a utilitarian fibre-cement roofing product over a long period of time (including stints outside to see how it would weather). Vertical articulation was achieved using a standard roofing ridge piece, a cornice detail through the repurposing of an apron flashing piece, and cills from cutting and shaping a coping piece. In this instance, Sugarhouse Studios provided the space for testing and making adaptations to more affordable and often industrial products not commonly specified due to their aesthetic qualities. However, by combining these standard components with a few bespoke elements – in the model the plaster mouldings and stainless-steel clips – a new hybrid system was formed.

Assemble,
Sugarhouse Studios,
Stratford,
London,
2014

Sugarhouse Studios enables members of the collective to experiment with a number of different materials in the same space simultaneously.

It is this hybridity that characterises research in Assemble's practice, whereby constant experimentation in the studio encourages the discovery of more unusual solutions

Assemble shares tools and workshop facilities in its studio with over 50 other makers, organised around an open space prioritised for large-scale production.

Building Together

It is this hybridity that characterises research in Assemble's practice, whereby constant experimentation in the studio encourages the discovery of more unusual solutions, mindful that good design does not require expensive materials. This methodology also acknowledges that design is often a double articulation between a more or less linear process that necessitates the production of a singular object, yet that it exists always in tension with unknown contingencies discovered along the way. In Assemble's work, this is catalysed by the multiplicity of voices within such a large collective. Its approach therefore prioritises the space needed for such experimentation, encouraging the pursuit of open-ended paths, which often result in mistakes more than the consolidation of a design. The cost of the studio is thus an integral part of the collective's business strategy, with the value of making factored into both design briefs and fee proposals. In fact, in many projects it is the process of making that is the focus of the design itself, with the object-based outcome contingent on an agreed strategy rather than a predetermined form to which materials are applied.

The value of Sugarhouse Studios also lies in its ability, as a space, to give visibility to fabrication techniques within an environment shared with other creative tenants. Observing individual skills in action on a daily basis creates moments for collaboration, engendering links to be made across several disciplines, which pushes the individual limits of both material and maker. Long-term working relationships are fostered in close proximity, meaning that while Assemble's work is increasingly being produced in the context of an office environment, someone else within Sugarhouse Studios is often involved in the realisation of the design. Therefore, rather than adopting a singular notion of what constitutes materials research as such, Assemble has devised an infrastructure that supports time, space and sociality for experimentation to take place. This approach coheres within a discourse that thinks about how making processes empower people to comprehend the socioeconomic conditions of design. As such it establishes criticality around the sustainability of constructing alternative forms of working that are considered extrinsic to the profession, experimenting instead with how to coexist within a constellation of rapidly changing forms of building practices. ᴅ

Rather than adopting a singular notion of what constitutes materials research as such, Assemble has devised an infrastructure that supports time, space and sociality for experimentation to take place

Text © 2019 John Wiley & Sons Ltd. Images: © Assemble

Translating Culture

Martyn Hook

Framing Indigenous Knowledge Through Architecture

Lyons Architecture, iredale pedersen hook and ASPECT Studios,
Yagan Square,
Perth, Western Australia,
2018

above: Yagan Square, named after an early Noongar leader, is a major cultural and civic centre for Perth's new City Link Precinct. The design team collaborated with the local Whadjuk Noongar community to reflect the communities' aspirations in the design of the urban place.

left: Yagan Square creates a large 'gathering place' for all people of Western Australia, shaded by an expansive canopy that seeks to share Indigenous knowledge through ceremony and through stories of the land, by bringing Indigenous and non-Indigenous people, traditional owners and visitors to 'Country' (as Indigenous Australians refer to their homeland) to build consciousness towards reconciliation and acknowledgment of sovereignty.

Can architecture contribute to equality and reconciliation of indigenous peoples? Having worked with Aboriginal communities for over two decades on a series of typologies across Western Australia, architects iredale pedersen hook have recently contributed to a major scheme for the heart of Perth's central business district. Yagan Square's spatial framework is informed by the substantial historical research and public engagement that are at the heart of their method, bringing Indigenous and non-Indigenous people together. **Martyn Hook**, a co-director of the practice and Dean of the School of Architecture and Urban Design at Melbourne's RMIT University, explains.

iredale pedersen hook's architecture seeks to embody a unique design response to the environmental and social context in which the projects are situated. The firm's involvement in the completion in 2018 of Yagan Square in Perth can be viewed as the culmination of a research trajectory in the translation of an understanding of West Australian Indigenous culture into a major new public space in the city and perhaps signals a 'normalising' of the presence of Aboriginal culture in everyday lives.

Located at the east end of the new City Link development and constructed on land reclaimed by the sinking of a railway line, Yagan Square is a major investment in the cultural and civic infrastructure of the city. Produced in deep collaboration with Lyons Architecture, landscape architects ASPECT Studios, the Whadjuk Working Party (a representative body of local traditional landowners) and Professor Paul Carter, alongside a collection of local artists, the design responds to the imperative for Yagan Square to be an inclusive, welcoming and active cultural and civic destination, representative of a diversity of the local Perth region and broader Western Australia.

The project is underpinned by the ideas of convergence: convergence of geologies, tracks, narratives, Indigenous and non-Indigenous people and culture within the Square. The team used historical research and extensive public engagement towards the aim to devise a spatial framework capable of mitigating the current tensions between Indigenous and non-Indigenous, in the respect of history and traditions as well as creating a new functional transport node and public space for the city.

iredale pedersen hook,
Observation of existing patterns,
Tjuntjuntjara,
Western Australia,
2008

iredale pedersen hook,
New community housing –
supporting existing
patterns,
Tjuntjuntjara,
Western Australia,
2008

New community houses were designed to support observed living patterns, and post-occupancy photographs were utilised to record and decode resultant space usage.

Following an anthropological approach, the architects utilised photographs to capture and decode Indigenous community living patterns throughout the seasons.

Closing the Gap

Despite direct Federal Government policy, the Indigenous people of Australia still have life expectancy of 10 years less than non-Indigenous Australians, only around 50 per cent of Indigenous kids go to school, remote communities are often riddled with alcohol abuse and violence, and the Indigenous population is grossly over-represented in Australian prisons.[1] Architecture that is culturally aware can play a role in facilitating solutions to these critical problems but cannot contribute appropriately without substantial research in practice.

For over twenty years, iredale pedersen hook (IPH) have been working with Aboriginal communities in the North West of Australia in housing, children's centres, health facilities, language centres, an elders centre, a courthouse and even a prison. Through the progression of building typologies, the practice has built a way of working with community and government that collects strategy, deep consultation (often with anthropologists), careful observation, procurement, operation and post-occupancy evaluation into a coherent body of research that builds with each project undertaken.

Consideration of the IPH research through practice that informed Yagan Square is captured in a drawing that explores the most prominent projects assembled as a 'continuum' rather than a linear progression. Aspects of the projects inform each other but it is through the reading of a collective cultural AND architectural interrogation of the work that IPH see its value in research; that is, the doing of the architecture assists in the understanding of its impact on the awareness and translations of Aboriginal culture in the creation of built form. Each project requires a unique perspective as it is Indigenous-led from the outset and other considerations are secondary, with climatic durability and remote construction as high priorities. For example, the West Kimberley Regional Prison in Derby (2012; designed with TAG Architects) is assembled as a community of language groups through clustered houses around a football oval, with clear views to sacred landmarks framed by the architecture. Walumba Elders Centre in Warmun (2012) seeks to be respectful of private cultural activities that are gender-specific, with its roof form shifting to conceal activity, but also to celebrate transmission of knowledge through community traditions of cooking kangaroo or the arrival of the rains with expressive, massive gutters.

The doing of the architecture assists in the understanding of its impact on the awareness and translations of Aboriginal culture in the creation of built form

iredale pedersen hook with TAG Architects,
West Kimberley Regional Prison,
Derby, Western Australia,
2012

above: The architects worked in collaboration with the local Indigenous community to design a culturally appropriate prison for the Aboriginal people of the remote Kimberley region in Western Australia.

iredale pedersen hook,
Walumba Elders Centre,
Warmun, Western Australia,
2012

below: The local Gija people led the design of a culturally appropriate age-care building in the remote community of Warmun after devastating floods struck the town and forced residents off their homeland. The centre is a place for the community to meet with their elders and for the ongoing teaching of Indigenous lore and culture.

Increasingly projects across Australia such as Yagan Square have an explicit obligation to engage and promote Aboriginal culture with non-Indigenous communities

iredale pedersen hook,
Indigenous Collections,
2018

Watercolour illustration depicting works by iredale pedersen hook architects which encompass design concepts that have emerged over 20 years of working with Indigenous communities in the far North West of Australia.

An Architecture of Extremes

Indigenous Australians are the custodians of the oldest continuous culture on Earth, having occupied this landscape for 60,000 years. Increasingly projects across Australia such as Yagan Square have an explicit obligation to engage and promote Aboriginal culture with non-Indigenous communities. It is challenging to produce architecture in remote and regional communities under extreme climatic conditions and in the context of extreme cultural complexity, but the reward now is the translation of this knowledge into a large-scale urban project. In practice-based research the architectural idea is intrinsically linked to the generation of new knowledge through its 'application', and it is at this point that the intersection with Indigenous culture is critical in that the architecture becomes a tool that the community can use to pass on their knowledge through generations of Indigenous and non-Indigenous Australians along with visitors to Whadjuk Country, making the richness of their culture tangible. ∆

Note
1. See 'Close the Gap: Indigenous Health Campaign', Australian Human Rights Commission website, 8 February 2018: www.humanrights.gov.au/our-work/aboriginal-and-torres-strait-islander-social-justice/projects/close-gap-indigenous-health; and 'FactCheck Q&A: Are Indigenous Australians the Most Incarcerated People on Earth?', The Conversation website, 6 June 2017: http://theconversation.com/factcheck-qanda-are-indigenous-australians-the-most-incarcerated-people-on-earth-78528.

Text © 2019 John Wiley & Sons Ltd. Images: pp 108, 109, 112 © Peter Bennetts; pp 110–11, 113 © iredale pedersen hook architects

Deborah Saunt, Tom Greenall and Roberta Marcaccio

COLLECTIVE IMPRESSIONS OF SMITHSON PLAZA

WEAVING HISTORY WITH THE PRESENT

Economist Plaza,
London,
1964 and 2016

Views from Bury Street, across the plaza towards St James's Street.
Opposite left: Original design by the Smithsons photographed by Michael Carapetian in 1964.
Middle: The space as it appeared in 2016 after SOM's alterations were carried out in 1990.
Below: DSDHA's proposed areas of intervention (in red) to 'edit out' the elements that have departed from the Smithsons' original design intent.

Designed by Alison and Peter Smithson in the early 1960s, the former Economist Plaza in London is an icon of the modern movement. Its recent restoration by architectural firm DSDHA drew on the Smithsons' own post-occupancy appraisals, as well as consultation with scholars who revealed the complex's choreographed nature. What was initially a retrofit with environmental performance enhancements thus evolved into a strategy to reinstate lost dynamism. Guest-Editors **Deborah Saunt, Tom Greenall and Roberta Marcaccio** – all key members of the DSDHA team – tell its story.

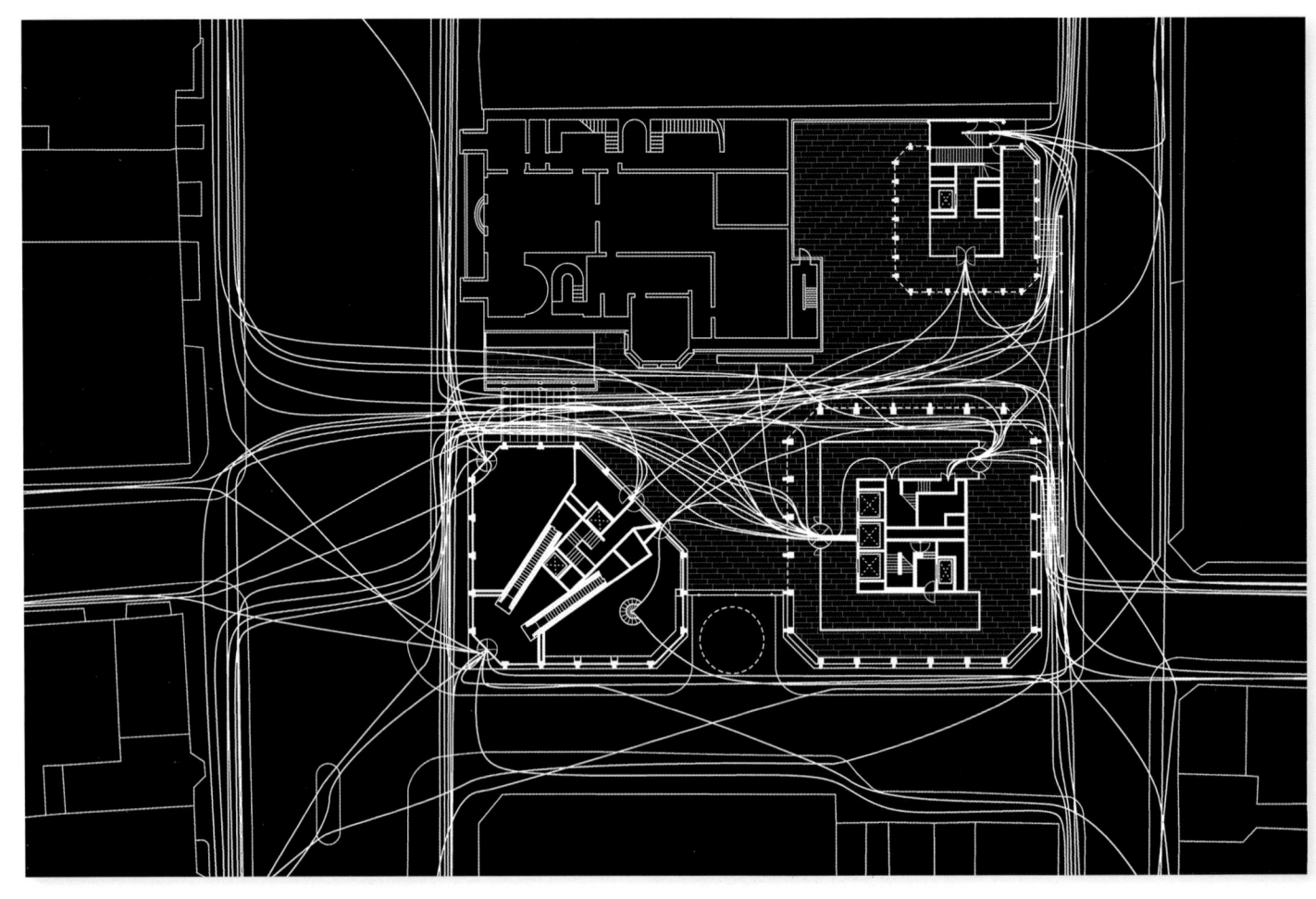

DSDHA,
Economist Plaza movement analysis,
London, 2016

above: DSDHA's movement analysis of the plaza as it was intended by the Smithsons in 1964, upon completion of their project.
opposite: Movement analysis of the space after SOM's reworking in 1990. DSDHA's design proposals aimed to transform the plaza's choreography of movement to bring back its original dynamism.

After its completion in 1964, Alison and Peter Smithson continually revisited the Economist Plaza to make new appraisals which they then crystallised in writing, drawing and photographs. As part of their restoration of the complex (now renamed Smithson Plaza), DSDHA studied these documents closely, alongside other existing literature, and conducted first-hand research on the ground, observing how people occupy and move through the space. All this informed their project, the first phase of which was completed in July 2018 and has seen the plaza resurfaced, with new lobbies for both the residential and office towers. Four floors of the residential tower have been retrofitted and six floors of the office tower were renovated to create approximately 2,000 square metres (21,530 square feet) of Grade A work spaces. The latter's environmental performance was enhanced through the installation of new double-glazed windows, insulation and discreet new services and lifts. At street level the scheme has created a new art gallery, while a public art programme has been reintroduced at the plaza level to revive the long and established tradition of the space as a prominent stage for London's creative scene.

Change: An Idea to Keep
One of London's most beloved architectural icons, the Economist Plaza featured prominently in journals, history books, fashion shoots and cult films such as Michelangelo Antonioni's *Blow-Up* (1966). In 1988, it was Grade II* listed, and for the past 50 years has been a compulsory destination for any architectural student interested in the modern movement. As such both the architectural community and town planners were quite sceptical of any suggested alteration. To establish a constructive dialogue, DSDHA studied the Smithsons' attitude towards change. In their writings the duo described the Plaza as an open-ended, highly flexible set of buildings composed of elements with both long-term and short-term lifespans. The former are 'permanent' design gestures that have impact at an urban scale and as such resist change. The latter are instead 'transient' elements – like the technological appliances or prefabricated components – that can be replaced more regularly when a new technology becomes available or new uses require new configurations.

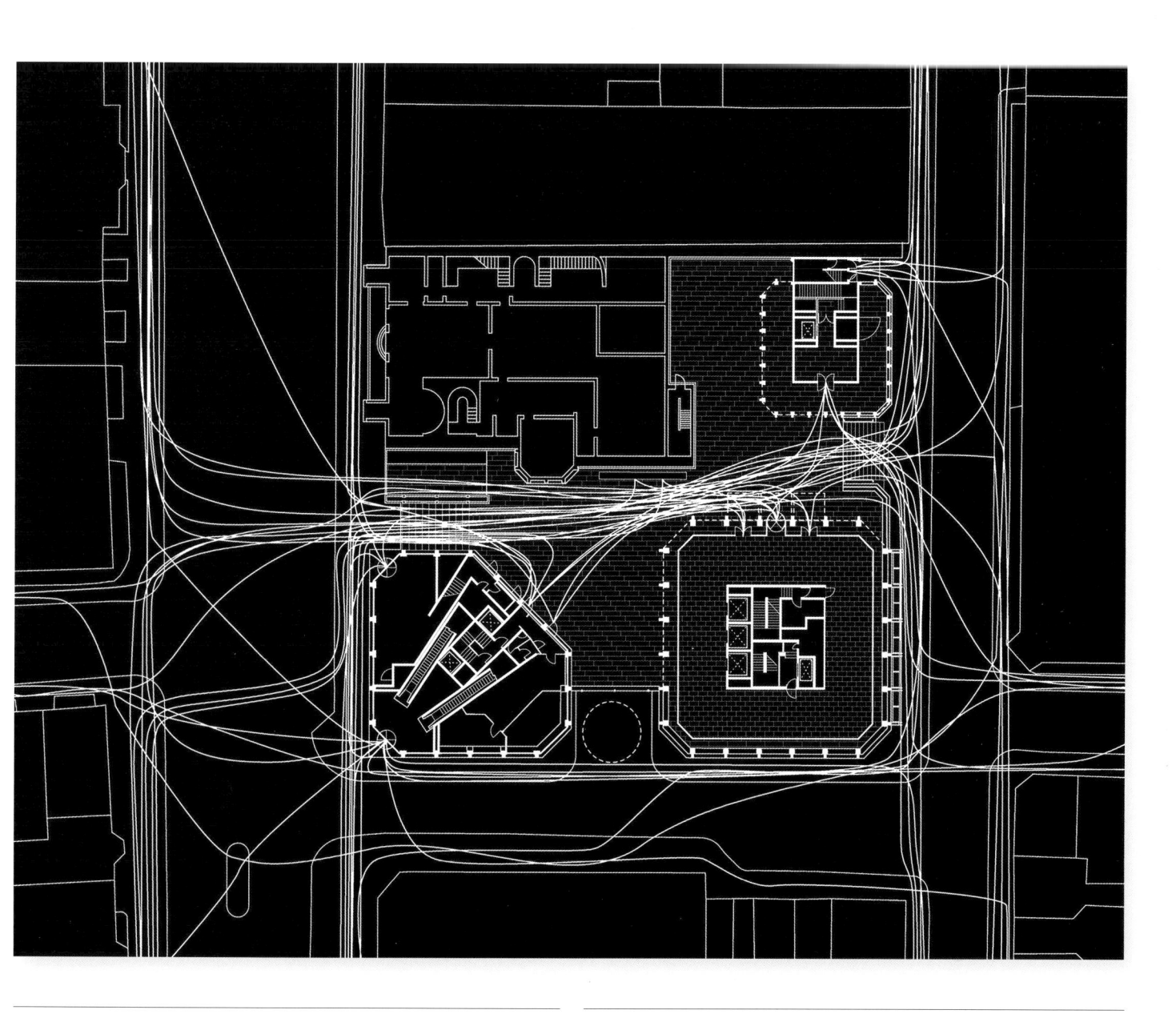

Faithful to these principles, the Smithsons themselves carried out alterations to the entrance of the office tower in 1984, when having been a headquarters for one single organisation, the building became a multi-tenanted block. Further and clearly less successful changes occurred in the 1990s during Skidmore, Owings & Merrill's major reworking of the complex, which included the expansion of the office lobby into the colonnade, the remodelling of the stepped access to the plaza on Bury Street, and a series of extensions on the same prospect. Moreover, the bank occupying the lowest of the three blocks departed and a restaurant took over, latterly fitted out by Kenzo Kuma with dark tinted windows that have destroyed the building's visual permeability. DSDHA mapped these little-known alterations, distinguishing those in keeping with the Smithsons' visions from those that departed from it and therefore needed to be addressed in the new scheme.

A Choreography of Movements
In conversation with distinguished scholars (Professors Susannah Hagan from Westminster University, and Max Risselada and Dirk van den Heuvel from the Delft University of Technology), DSDHA uncovered that the Smithsons had conceived their three buildings as elements of the townscape, to be experienced kinetically according to a precise choreography of movements and views towards and through the cluster. DSDHA then mapped the original patterns of movement and revealed how the intrinsic dynamism of the complex was subtly eroded by each subsequent change. The result was that the plaza had become less vital, and this public space's celebrated quietude had mutated into an efficient thoroughfare towards the office tower with undesirable views into the restaurant's back-of-house. The aim of the new scheme was to restore this lost dynamism and define an urban choreography more attuned to the 21st century.

To this end, DSDHA also catalogued the photographs the Smithsons had commissioned for their multiple accounts of their project. The team established the exact location from which the views had been taken and mapped their cones of visibility to identify the extent of the complex captured by each image. The aim was to establish a visual/spatial hierarchy, distinguishing the most iconic views – elements to be restored to the

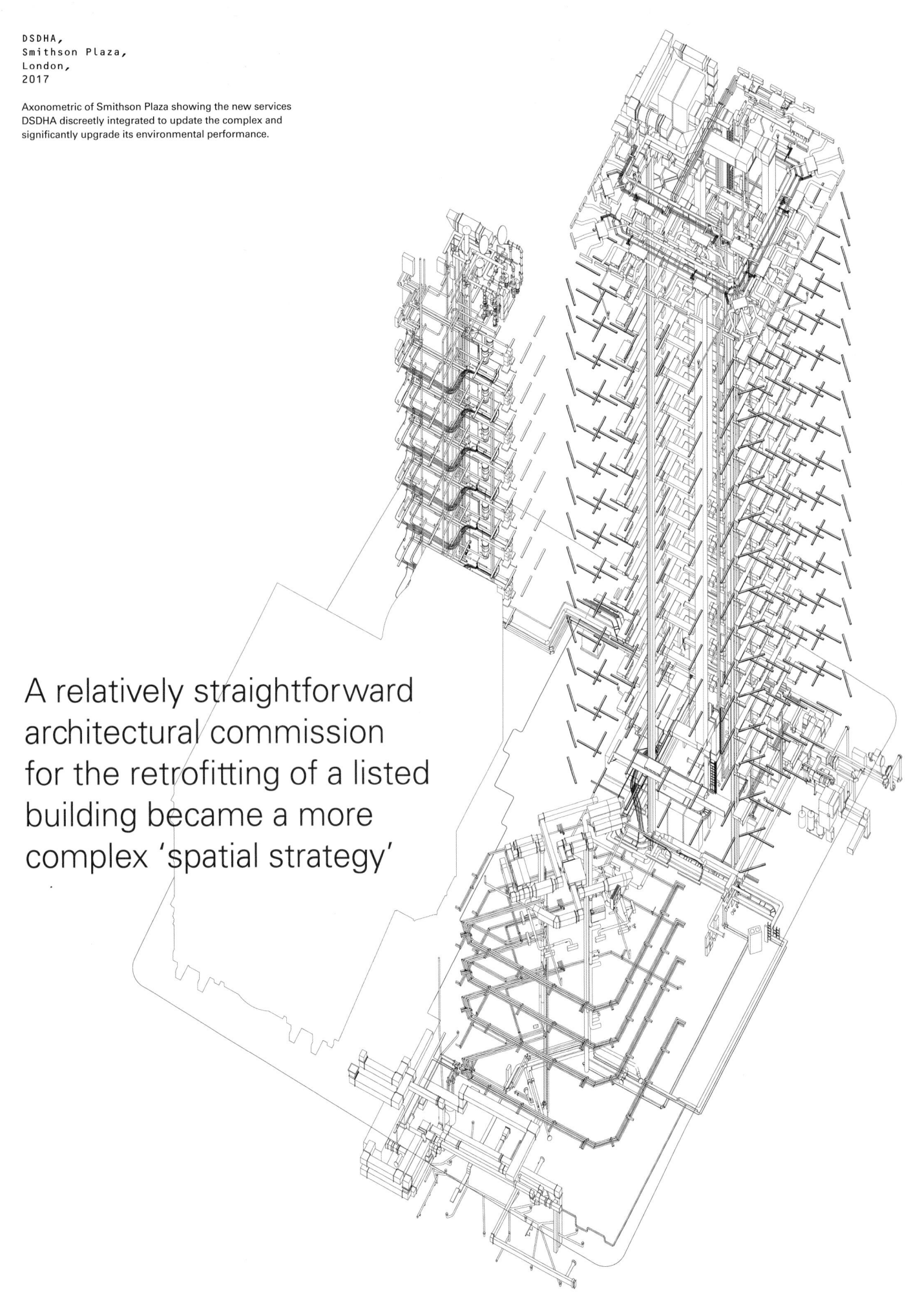

DSDHA,
Smithson Plaza,
London,
2017

Axonometric of Smithson Plaza showing the new services DSDHA discreetly integrated to update the complex and significantly upgrade its environmental performance.

A relatively straightforward architectural commission for the retrofitting of a listed building became a more complex 'spatial strategy'

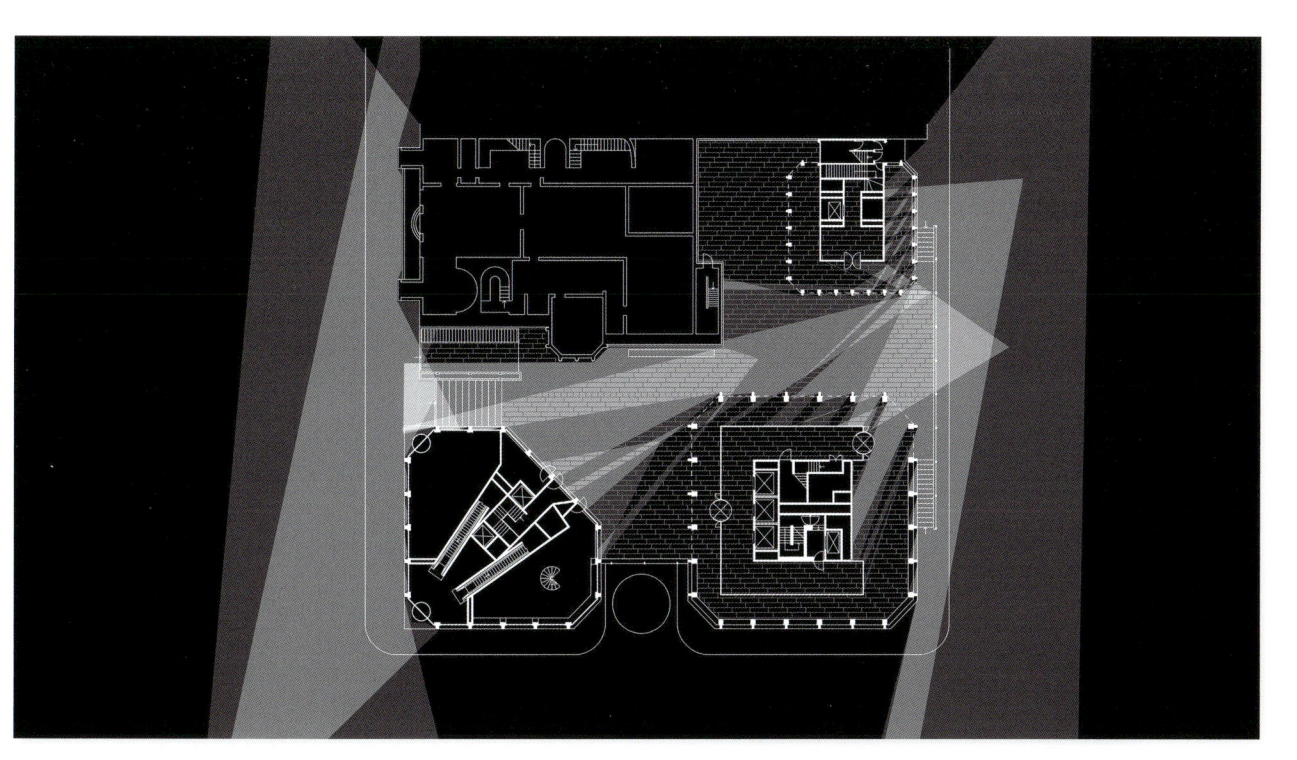

DSDHA,
Overlay of historical views of the Economist Plaza,
London,
2016

Having catalogued the photographs the Smithsons themselves had commissioned and/or published, DSDHA established the exact location from which each had been taken and mapped their cones of visibility before overlaying them onto the original plan from 1964. In so doing, the practice could identify areas which, having not been featured in any of the publications curated by the Smithsons, were perhaps less significant in townscape terms, and, as such, could be updated to meet the demands of contemporary office, gallery and public space.

DSDHA,
Smithson Plaza,
London,
2018

The DSDHA team on the plaza after its recent renovation. From left to right: Eleanor Alexander, Martin Pearson, Robert Eaton, Roberta Marcaccio, Sanket Ghatalia, Deborah Saunt and David Hills.

original design intent as much as possible for their importance in townscape terms – from the lesser-known and perhaps less successful angles, where the complex could be updated to meet the demands of contemporary office, gallery and public space. This led to the proposal to turn the carpark entrance on Ryder Street, which does not appear in any historical photos, into a gallery space and, in future phases of the project, insert a new discreet staircase that will make the raised plaza accessible to the south.

Through these research methods, DSDHA could debunk the myth of the Economist Plaza as an untouchable icon. The practice's methodologies acted as a rhetorical tool to substantiate hunches, but moreover allowed a series of discoveries that guided the design, even steering the project beyond its initial scope. In this way a relatively straightforward architectural commission for the retrofitting of a listed building became a more complex 'spatial strategy' that encompassed elements of the urban landscape, and evolved as a bespoke response to the heritage value of the building to inject new life into the city. DSDHA's historical research and related design tools are now informing new projects as well as becoming the subject of academic papers and lectures that will hopefully further studies of the Smithsons' work. ᴅ

Text © 2019 John Wiley & Sons Ltd. Images: p 114(l) © Michael Carapetian Photographer; pp 114–15(c), 115(r), 116–17, 118, 119(t) © DSDHA; p 119(b) © Luca Miserocchi

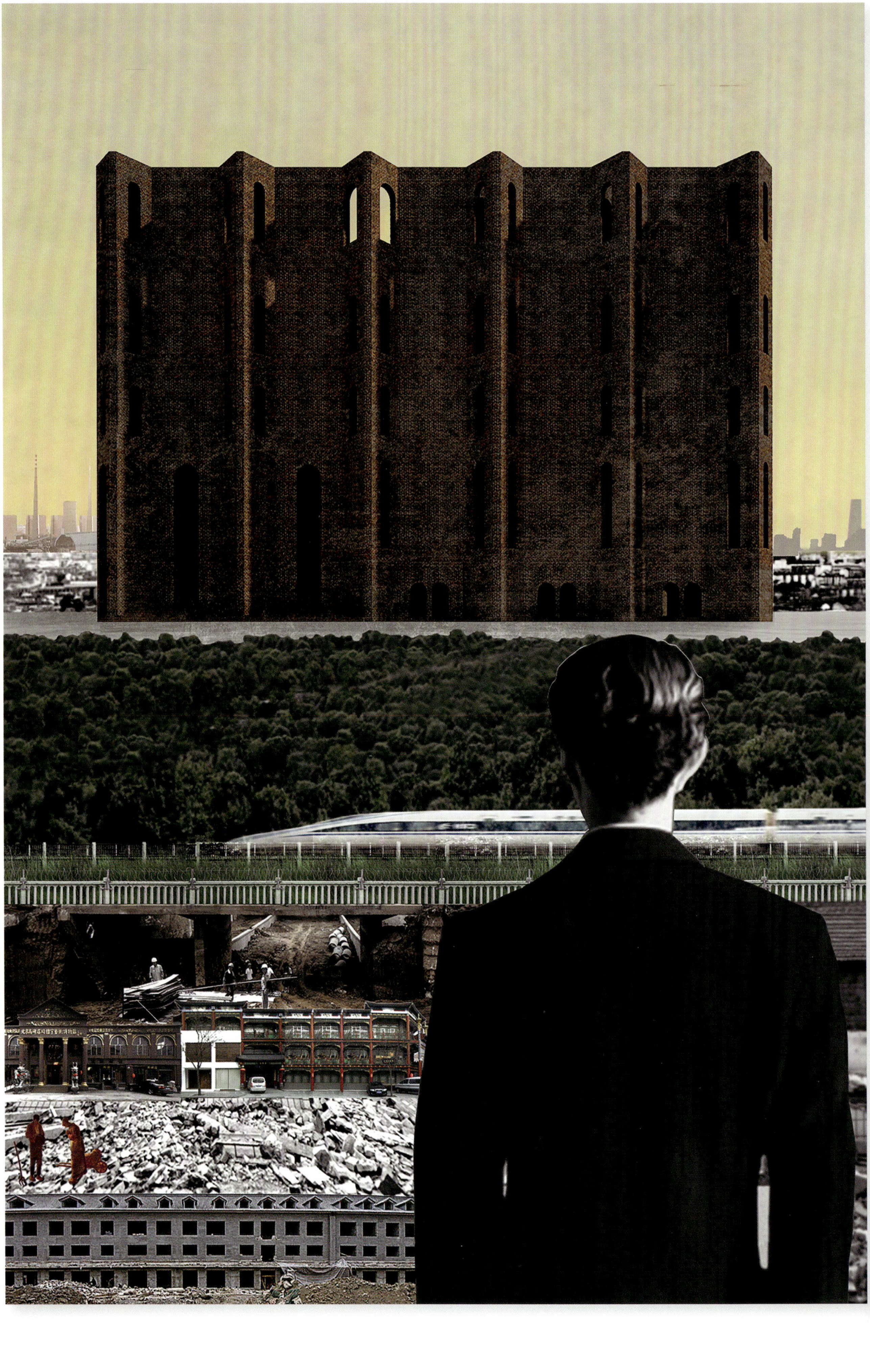

John Zhang

Towards a New Normal

The Blurred Landscape of Architectural Research in China

THANLAB,
Chinese Academy of Oil Painting,
Beijing,
2017

Research-led design for an artistic enclave, set against the unstoppable progress of urban expansion in Beijing.

The legacy of the Soviet era and 40 years of market-led reform have given the Chinese architectural profession a unique profile. Architect and researcher **John Zhang,** who teaches a China-focused studio at the University of Westminster in London, sets out its three main strands, each of which blends domains that are largely separate in the West. From state-owned Local Design Institutes often affiliated to universities, to commercial developers with in-house design capabilities, to a new generation of theoretically engaged architects who use their practice as means to establish their critical positions, he investigates their genealogy and approaches, and explores their pros and cons as models of architectural practice.

Architectural research within academia, practice and the market is often perceived to be taking place in isolation, despite the pressure on these ever-shrinking 'islands' to be more communicative and valuable to each other. To this end China offers a global and non-Eurocentric counterpoint, where architectural research is increasingly taking place over a blurred landscape that straddles the three domains.

Between Academia and Practice

In contrast to the UK model, architectural research and pedagogy in China does not exist in an isolated academia, but is exposed to the world of practice via university-affiliated state-owned architectural practices.

This is largely a legacy of the era under China's first Communist leader Mao Zedong (1949–76) when Soviet models shaped the forms of expression, the means of professional practice and the structure of pedagogy in Chinese architecture. Architecture schools became a part of the state apparatus, and the profession was nationalised into a system of state-owned practices, better known today in the West as Local Design Institutes (LDIs).

With matters of style beyond debate (China having already adopted wholesale Soviet-influenced Socialist Realism), architecture research and pedagogy became more practically and technically focused, which logically led to the birth of the university-affiliated LDIs, operated by architecture schools themselves. In the post-Mao era, thanks largely to market-oriented reforms and a professional regulatory system skewed heavily in their favour, the LDIs and their affiliation with architecture schools have survived the collapse of the Soviet paradigm. Today, some of the largest and most prominent practices in China are LDIs, and some of the most prominent LDIs are still affiliates of the most renowned Chinese architecture schools.

Such a relationship between academia and practice presents a series of perceived advantages for those in the West who wish for a closer proximity between teaching, research and practice. The income from the LDI contributes towards greater financial independence and funding for the development of practical knowledge as well as more theoretical, historical and reflective inquiries, which are so often underfunded. In reciprocity, university-affiliated LDIs can also gain a broader spectrum and greater depth of knowledge, making them more competitive. From a pedagogical perspective, the exposure to and immersion in the professional environment of the LDI provide students with precious experience of the realities of practice.

To a certain extent, this is indeed the case with Tongji University and its affiliate LDI, Tongji Architecture Design Group (TJAD), whose success is built upon the rich history of cross-pollination of knowledge and expertise with the university, where many of the TJAD architects are also academics undertaking teaching, research and practice activities simultaneously. Reciprocally, a significant amount of the university's research output is directly commissioned by TJAD, which often takes the form of consultative research as part of live projects, further blurring the boundary between research and practice. Pedagogically, many of the students from the school are interns at TJAD, and go on to become employees at the LDI, which remains a popular destination for graduates, despite the appeal of foreign architects and boutique design-led studios. With such retention of talent, TJAD has also become the incubator for some of China's new generation of more critically engaged design talents, such as Atelier Deshaus, whose principal directors both studied at Tongji University and worked at TJAD.

However, it would be naive to think that such a model is without flaws. Architects in university-affiliated LDIs are expected to be income generators for the practice to prosper, while simultaneously contributing to teaching and researching hours within the school. When the management structure of education, research and practice overlap under the same ambiguous institutional umbrella, the commercial impetus inevitably competes with the pedagogical and research priorities of academia. Consequently, the method and purpose of architectural education and research can be prone to distortion. This is evident in the nature of many supposedly research-led Master's degrees in Chinese architecture schools, where the students spend a significant amount of their time working for their supervisors as interns, in an exchange between cheap labour and the possibility of job security in a state enterprise.

Tongji Architectural Design (TJAD),
TJAD New Office Building,
Shanghai,
China,
2011

Whilst still affiliated to Tongji University, TJAD has become one of China's most prominent state-owned architectural practices, with its own premises outside of the campus, in a remodelled bus station.

Between Market and Practice

In another departure from the Western paradigm, real-estate developers have also become drivers of architectural research in China, increasingly circumventing the architect in the design process.

This is a unique consequence of the rapid formation and growth of the Chinese property development market in the reform era. Having emerged in the late 1980s, the first generation of Chinese real-estate developers initially modelled their operations on their nearest professionalised counterparts in Hong Kong and Singapore, quickly finding that they needed more nuanced and locally specific responses to the particular demands of the domestic market. However, they discovered that the architectural profession, at least in the early 1990s, was not quite ready to meet their expectations. The handful of foreign architects who had entered China at the time lacked a full understanding of the complexities of the domestic market and the subtleties of the pattern of demand in China. On the other hand, the archaic LDIs were still undergoing reforms themselves to shake off their Soviet past, lacking the knowledge and experience to produce market-led solutions in sectors that often did not exist in pre-reform China.

In this knowledge gap, Chinese developers were forced to become self-reliant by recruiting and forming their own team of architects and designers to offer in-house design capabilities, in order to meet the challenges of the market and the rapid pace of development. As that pace continued to increase and the market became ever more competitive in the 2000s, maturing developers have further consolidated their design expertise and capabilities, formalising their research and development operations.

The vast research base in Dongguan, Guangzhou, by Vanke, one of China's largest property developers, exemplifies this consolidation of research on the developer side.[1] On a site of 130,000 square metres (1.4 million square feet), the Vanke Architecture Research Centre comprises a series of research and public-engagement facilities in a campus landscape designed by Chinese architecture firm Z+T Studio. The on-site buildings, with the exception of the zero-carbon centre designed by GBBN, are designed in-house by Vanke itself. Hosting developer-led research that feeds directly back into the business, the site contains labs to test the performance of various exterior and interior materials, along with a plethora of research spaces set aside for collaboration with various universities' postdoctoral research programmes. With an increasing proportion of Vanke's construction utilising prefabrication, a large factory workshop space is provided for the prototyping and testing of prefabricated building elements, whilst another area showcases full-size prefabricated prototype housing units with internal layouts and finishes fully installed. A full-scale structural concrete shell tower replicates the conditions of a residential high-rise, used to test drainage, air-conditioning and firefighting systems in-situ. The campus is run on sustainable energy, processed on site, which also hosts a Zero Carbon Centre aimed at public engagement and education. The landscape contains ponds and wetlands that harvest rain and grey water from the site, clean them through filtration beds and feed back into the water supply system.

Vanke is not an anomaly. Nine of the 10 largest real-estate developers have some form of in-house design, research and development organisation.[2] As such, professional architects are increasingly excluded from the design process, particularly in the residential sector, which accounts for a substantial segment

Within this campus-like site, Vanke designed most of the buildings in-house, with exceptions of the external landscaping and the Zero Carbon Centre, which are by Z+T Studio and GBBN respectively.

Vanke / GBBN / Z+T Studio,
Vanke Architecture Research Centre,
Dongguan,
China,
2013

The prototype yard at the Vanke Architecture Research Centre, showing a segmental mock-up of a decorative concrete facade element.

of the total construction output in China. Architects have become 'window-dressers' in many cases. To the lament of many within the profession, and perhaps as a consequence of the research prowess developers now possess, increasing numbers of architectural graduates are now shunning the traditional career path and joining developers to become client-side designers. The consensus among them is that they are likely to have more control over design quality and it will be easier to affect more significant changes at a more strategic level by working for developers instead of practices.

Between Practice and Academia

Whilst the activities of academics and developers are encroaching into the traditional remit of the practitioner in China, a new generation of Chinese architects are conversely deploying their practice as a form of academic research, using the opportunities afforded to them through commissions to critically address the plethora of challenges that have emerged in the wake of almost four decades of breakneck economic growth.

From the likes of now internationally renowned home-grown auteurs such as Wang Shu and Chang Yung Ho, to younger provocateurs such as Zhang Ke from ZAO/standardarchitecture and Wang Zigeng of PILLS, what unites this diverse range of Chinese architects is a sense of 'criticality' in their different approaches, meaning an awareness of their practice within the wider historical condition of contemporary China, and a reflectivity, through their work, on their resistance, and negation of the system within which their practice takes place.[3] As such, their built and unbuilt projects can be understood as a form of research, at once theoretical and practical, through which they can establish their critical position or 'thesis'. The Chinese critic and curator Li Xiangning uses the term 'critical pragmatism'[4] to describe the endeavours of these avant-garde Chinese architects. This criticality stands in contrast to the 'post-criticality'[5] of many foreign architects working in China, who had to resort to a sense of pragmatism and compromise in order to reconcile their critical positions against working in a contradiction-laden system where Communist rule and hyper-capitalism both prevail.

It is also important to point out that this critical awareness does not exist only in the debate over history, identity and craft, as exemplified in Wang Shu's particular kind of architecture. There are an increasing number of Chinese architects whose interests lie beyond matters of stylistic expression, and in the effect globalisation and the capitalistic mode of production have had on the constituency of labour, as well as their socio-spatial needs.

One such architect is Han Tao, who teaches at the Central Academy of Fine Arts in Beijing, and runs his own studio THANLAB. Representative of this crop of practically minded theoreticians, or theoretically minded practitioners, Han believes that the solutions to China's urban spatial problems lie not in more critique, but in more action. Through his work at the Chinese Academy of Oil Painting over the last 10 years, Han has been exploring the exclave conditions of new forms of communities in contemporary China, as antithesis to the prevailing models of spatial production under state capitalism. In this regard, Han's thinking is influenced by the polemics of Pier Vittorio Aureli[6] – the architect and educator who co-founded the Brussels architectural practice Dogma. For Han Tao, his clients, a community of commercially successful oil painters, are a post-Fordian creative labour force, or 'Cultural Workers',[7] who are

ZAO / standardarchitecture,
Micro-Hutong,
Beijing,
2015

The Micro-Hutong project can be understood as a prototype exploring the possibility of intimate, high-density urban living.

actively engaged in affecting real changes, in order to craft and propagate cultural narratives which either serve to legitimise the status quo or reveal new possibilities.

For Han Tao, the change affected by his clients does not stem from their artistic output, but in their very presence in such exclave conditions on the urban–rural boundary. As such Han's architecture becomes the means through which this artist community inserts itself into and engages with the local community. Starting from ad-hoc conversions of ex-industrial buildings, the campus has grown to become a monastic collection of structures that draws its inspiration from traditional Beijing settlements, the Florence Charterhouse in Italy (established 1341) and Le Corbusier's Convent of Saint-Marie de la Tourette near Lyon in France (1961). The intellectual intensity in Han's work is evident, and an integral part of the development of his critical positions as an academic, where the built project is clearly a research thesis by practice.

Blurred Boundaries

These Chinese precedents show that research thrives when it ventures beyond its traditional confines of the ivory towers. Indeed, in the academic model of the London School of Architecture (see pp 32–7 of this issue), in the post-occupancy research of WeWork (pp 68–75) and in the polemic-driven practice of Assemble (pp 102–7), we are already seeing UK evidence of these endeavours, which blur the boundary between research in academia, practice and the market. However, the Chinese paradigm should also act as a caution, against academic and practice-based research becoming distorted by the market, in an increasingly overlapped landscape. ᴆ

Notes
1. Subsequent data on Vanke Architecture Research Centre is drawn from the author's field trip: see John Zhang, 'Towards a New Normal: The Relationship Between Foreign and Chinese Architects in Contemporary China', unpublished PhD thesis, Royal College of Art, London, 2018.
2. Data compiled by the author from the Annual Reports of respective property development companies as well as the China Index Academy, a part of National Bureau of Statistics.
3. Jianfei Zhu, 'Criticality in between China and the West', *The Journal of Architecture*, 10 (5), 2005, p 199.
4. Term coined by Li Xiangning as the curator of the 2016 Harvard Graduate School of Design autumn exhibition 'Towards a Critical Pragmatism: Contemporary Chinese Architecture'.
5. Jianfei Zhu, *Architecture of Modern China: A Historical Critique*, Routledge (Oxford), 2009, p 190.
6. See Pier Vittorio Aureli, *The Project of Autonomy: Politics and Architecture Within and Against Capitalism*, Princeton Architectural Press (New York), 2008.
7. Han Tao, He Ziming, 'Zhong Guo You Hua Yuan Shi Nian – Wen Hua Gong Ren, Fei Di Yu Cong Hui Gong Tong Ti Sheng Huo De Ke Neng Xing' ('Ten Years of the Chinese Academy of Oil Painting: Cultural Workers, Exclaves and a Return to the Possibility of Communal Life'), *Jian Zhu Ji Yi (Architectural Techniques)*, 11, 2017.

THANLAB,
Chinese Academy of Oil Painting,
Beijing,
2017

The Lecture Hall at the Chinese Academy of Oil Painting has become a gathering space not only for the enclave of artists but also for the local community.

Text © 2019 John Wiley & Sons Ltd. Images: pp 120, 125 Courtesy of THANLAB; pp 122–4 © John Zhang

Less Grey, More Black and White

Architecture Needs a Consistent Platform in Research

COUNTERPOINT

DAVID GREEN

COUNTERPOINT 03/2019 No 259

This issue of △ showcases a range of architectural research approaches that proudly distance themselves from institutionalism or established canons. But is this really the most constructive direction to be headed in – or should we be going the opposite way? **David Green**, Principal of London practice Perkins+Will and CEO of the firm's non-profit research arm AREA Research, argues the case for establishing an accepted methodology that would not limit progress but rather open up opportunities for interdisciplinary collaboration and measurable outcomes.

I have been thinking about the relationship between academic research and the practice of architecture for a very long time. In the winter of 1991 I completed my graduate studies, and by the spring of 1992 I was working as both a practitioner and teacher, a situation that lasted for over 20 years, during which I was constantly struck by the disconnect between the work being done by academic researchers and that being done in the office.

It was about this time in the early 1990s that much of the public funding for state universities in the US was significantly reduced, and they had to look elsewhere for funding. They looked to external sources to supplement their funding, primarily commercial and non-traditional government institutions. Architecture programmes followed suit, and in many of those more rigorous, and fully funded, research efforts emerged.

Firms Thinking about Research

As a result of this, professional firms started to develop ideas about how they might engage in some sort of research. There was a lot of discussion about how it would change the profession, make it more robust, more accountable, more profitable, and numerous other potential transformations. Now, more than 25 years on, we are still trying to figure out what this means.

Interestingly, this dilemma regarding the lack of clarity in the definition of 'research' is not prevalent in most other professions or areas of scientific investigation. Medicine, sociology and biology, for example, all share something that architecture does not: a strong consensus around methodologies and protocols for the research process itself. They have platforms for research and development that are lacking in architecture.

The Direction of Architectural Research

In their Introduction to this issue of 𝐷 (pp 6–13), the Guest-Editors explain that many of the essays included are attempts to move beyond canonical forms of research towards more sophisticated (I am unsure of the meaning of the word 'sophisticated' in this context) methods of investigation. But in reality, the practice of architecture has never really been involved in canonical, or scientific, research, at least not in the way others have. It seems much more appropriate that, as a profession, we might want to move in the opposite direction: towards a more deliberate canonical platform as a basis for the construction of a research methodology for architecture.

This illustrates an underlying bias towards individual, divergent thinking that is clearly demonstrated through the variation in the articles in the issue. It is not the failings or successes of the individual endeavours that is telling the real story here. It is the simple fact that even taken together it would be extremely difficult for one to understand the overarching, data-driven trends, outcomes and correlations among these efforts, especially if looking in from outside the profession. It is hard to imagine this series of articles ending up in a single issue of the *New England Journal of Medicine*, for instance. But there is no reason that this should be the case. The built environment has a significant impact on both personal and public health. We should be pushing a research agenda that answers questions about these and myriad cross-disciplinary issues that currently confront the built environment. This can only be done through the implementation of a systematic platform upon which research is conducted.

This platform already exists. Much academic research, even in the academe of architecture, follows a more precise methodology, and as a profession we can create this methodological consistency, but it will be extremely difficult. We are taught that original thinking, uniqueness and our gut feelings are things to be celebrated, but these are all antithetical to the dispassion of research methodologies. Methodologies, after all, are not supposed to give us answers; rather they tell us how to investigate and what rules to follow to ensure that our outcomes are both valid and also usable across disciplines. To this end, in 2008 Perkins+Will began producing its *Research Journal*, organised not around a single subject, but around a uniform protocol for submission of research papers. Externally peer-reviewed, it allows for a wide variety of investigations with minimal deviation.

A compelling example of a success in this area is Tombolo, supported by the spatial analysis research and consulting firm Space Syntax. Tombolo was formed through the Future Cities Catapult initiative, a three-year innovation project to improve cities through data analysis. The project pulled experts from across industry and academia to form a strong foundation of collaboration, transparency and knowledge exchange. All of its products and services relate to general research, but with the distinction of having a design-led approach. Importantly, one of the central products created, the Digital Connector platform, promotes a level of homogenisation of analytical outputs (based on previously designed city indexes) and consequently comparative analysis between different cities, practices and projects that is not often seen elsewhere.

Perkins+Will Research Journal,
Vol 5,
January 2013

The journal is governed by strict research protocols and consistent expectations. It publishes peer-reviewed articles from all corners of the profession, ranging from technical investigations of material performance, to an overview of how our laws shape planning and development outcomes.

catAPULT Future Cities   Space Syntax

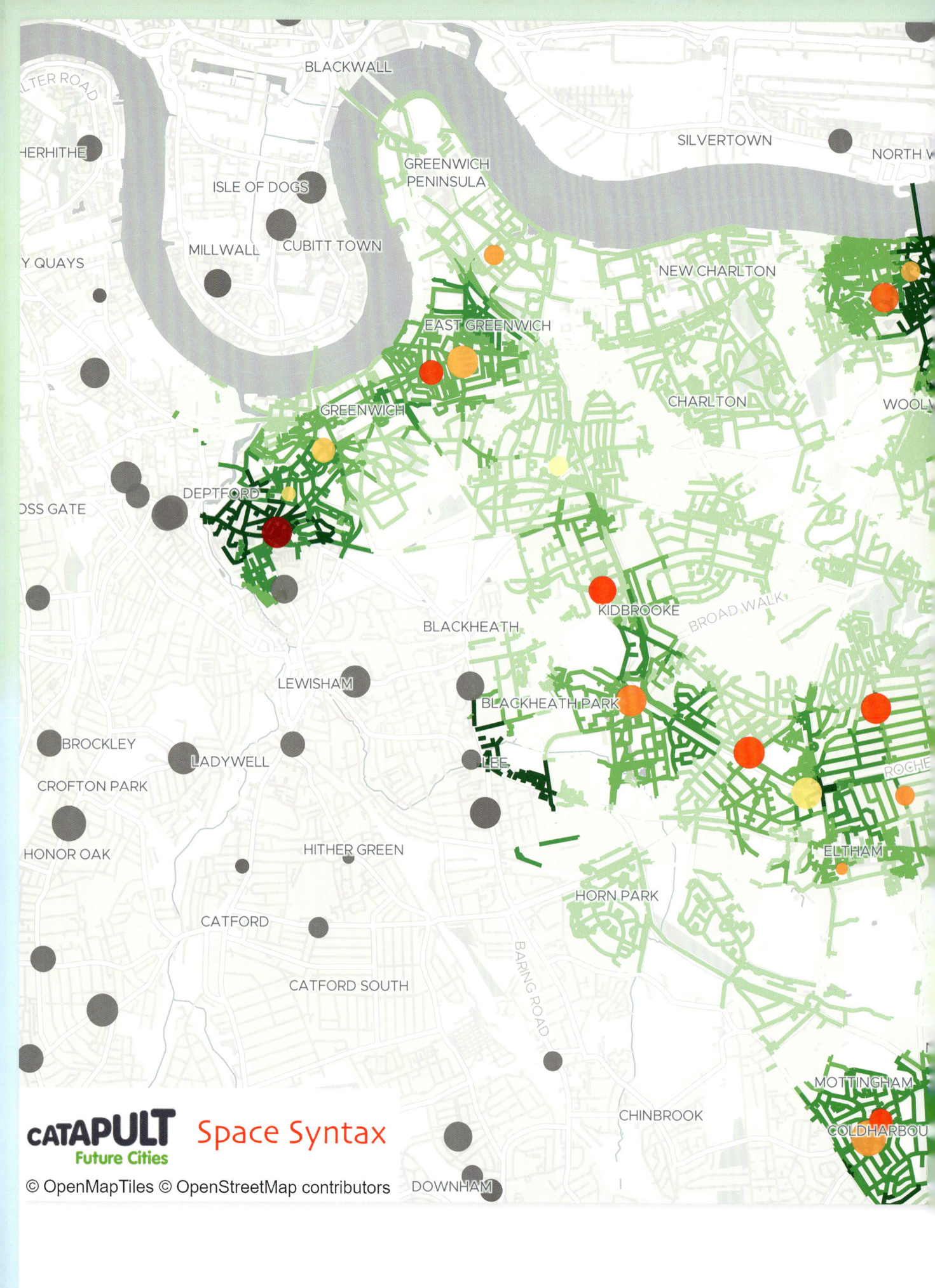

© OpenMapTiles © OpenStreetMap contributors

Tombolo Urban Data Explorer platform, 2018

Working through the government's Future Cities Catapult initiative, Tombolo created a set of tools to help designers and governments better understand the world through customisable data views and a standardised data platform. The image here maps journey times by different modes (walking, public transport and car) to General Practices for a number of districts. The visualisations also reveal both the quality of the NHS service and its physical accessibility, enabling identification of poorly served areas that can then be prioritised for future development action.

Methodologies, after all, are not supposed to give us answers; rather they tell us how to investigate and what rules to follow to ensure that our outcomes are both valid and also usable across disciplines

Aligning Architectural Research with Other Disciplines

When research is undertaken within a consistent framework, it opens up many more opportunities for interaction with other disciplines. Of interest here, for example, are our neurological reactions to various types of spaces and sequences. Why is it more comfortable, or comforting, to be near a wall when walking through a city than to be moving across a wide-open space? I suspect it is the result of our perception of time and how it seems to pass more quickly if one is walking close to a series of storefronts rather than in the middle of the desert. But lacking a consistent methodological platform for investigation, it is difficult to engage in a process that will produce data that indicate the veracity of this hypothesis. Of course, it is possible to do this, but the profession is yet to develop a platform that supports this effort in any meaningful way. We have not agreed on a consistent way to ask and answer the types of questions that influence the way people use the spaces we design, and which would deepen our understanding of their actual, real impact. I want a platform that allows me to engage in this research in partnership with directed neurological research, and I want this research to tell me if I am right or wrong.

Perkins+Will, Perceptions of Space and Time, Lexington and 32nd Street, New York, 2017

Why does walking half a mile cross-town in New York seem like a longer journey than walking half a mile uptown? One would gladly walk 10 blocks uptown to meet a friend for coffee, but three blocks cross-town is much less appealing.

Measuring Outcomes

Another challenge for architects at large, and one that is strangely counterintuitive, is our aversion to calculation for research purposes. Throughout this issue, there are minimal references to specific numeric outcomes for the various research efforts. And this is odd, because our entire existence as architects is centred on being able to measure things: rooms, column spacing, floor-to-ceiling heights and every other attribute of the built environment. But when asked to do this as part of a research project, particularly post-occupancy, we refuse. Most often the excuse is that the client will not pay for it, but this is simply a justification. Our profession is notorious for engaging in efforts for which we are not compensated, so this cannot be the explanation. There is something deeper here, almost a refusal to admit that we were wrong in our assumptions, that our design is somehow flawed. And, of course, this aversion to failure does not align with a specific research protocol. One of the basic tenets of research is that failure, and what that failure tells us, is as important as success. In this sense, I believe the Guest-Editors are correct in their observation that problems arise when research is subjected to the market and the impact of competition, appropriation and exploitation. These obstacles exist to some degree across all disciplines involved in research, but without a formal research methodology, and without rules, it is almost impossible to manage this situation in our own field.

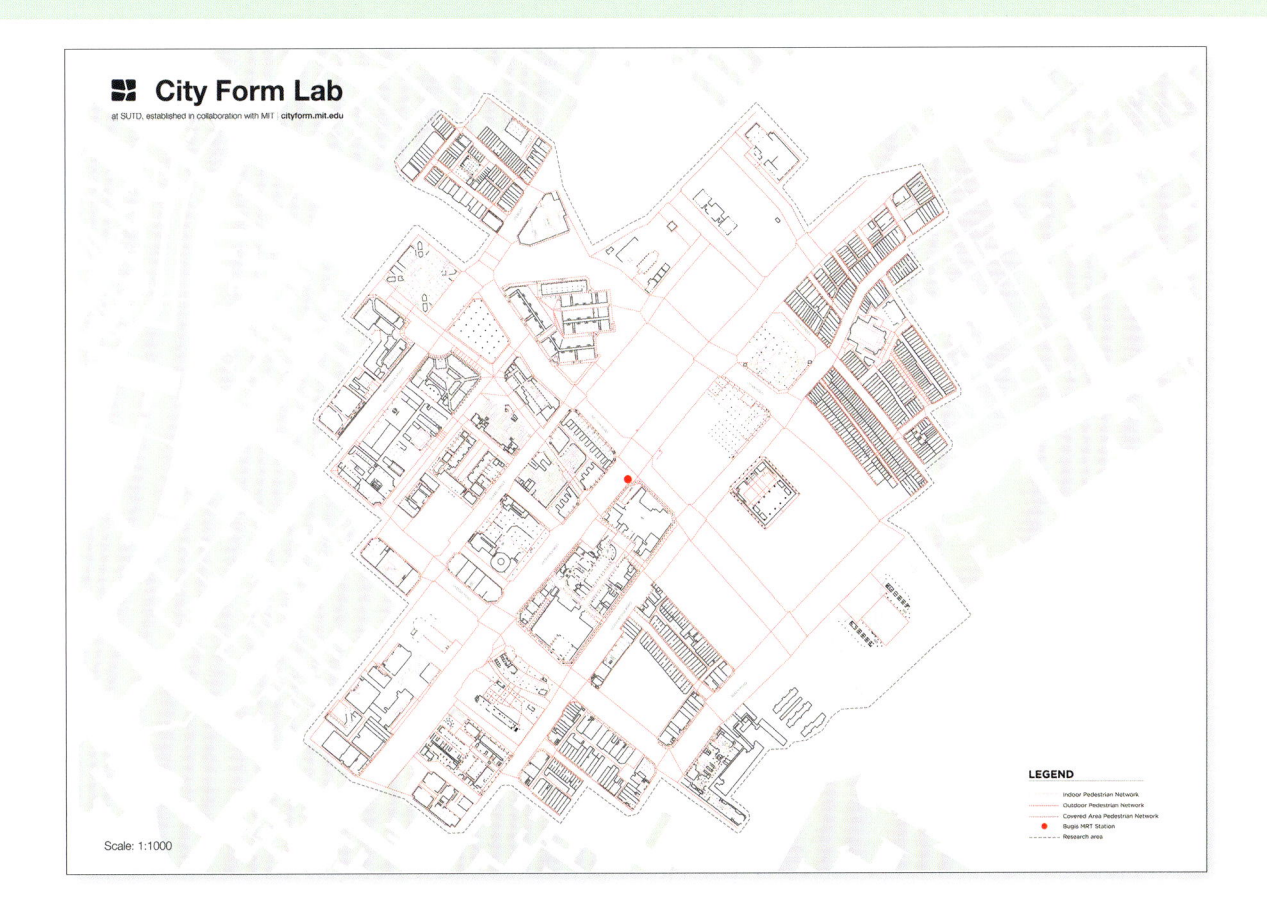

City Form Lab,
Samples of Urban Fabric in Singapore: comparative
geospatial data analysis of Bugis and Punggol,
Singapore University of Technology and Design (SUTD),
2013

Data collected within 10 minutes' walking distance from the Bugis underground Mass Rapid Transit and Meridian Light Rail Transit in Punggol. This kind of analytical comparison is useful to understand final outputs from districts with different characters. Bugis presents a mix of historical dendritic-patterned neighbourhoods with new office developments while Punggol is a mainly residential area.

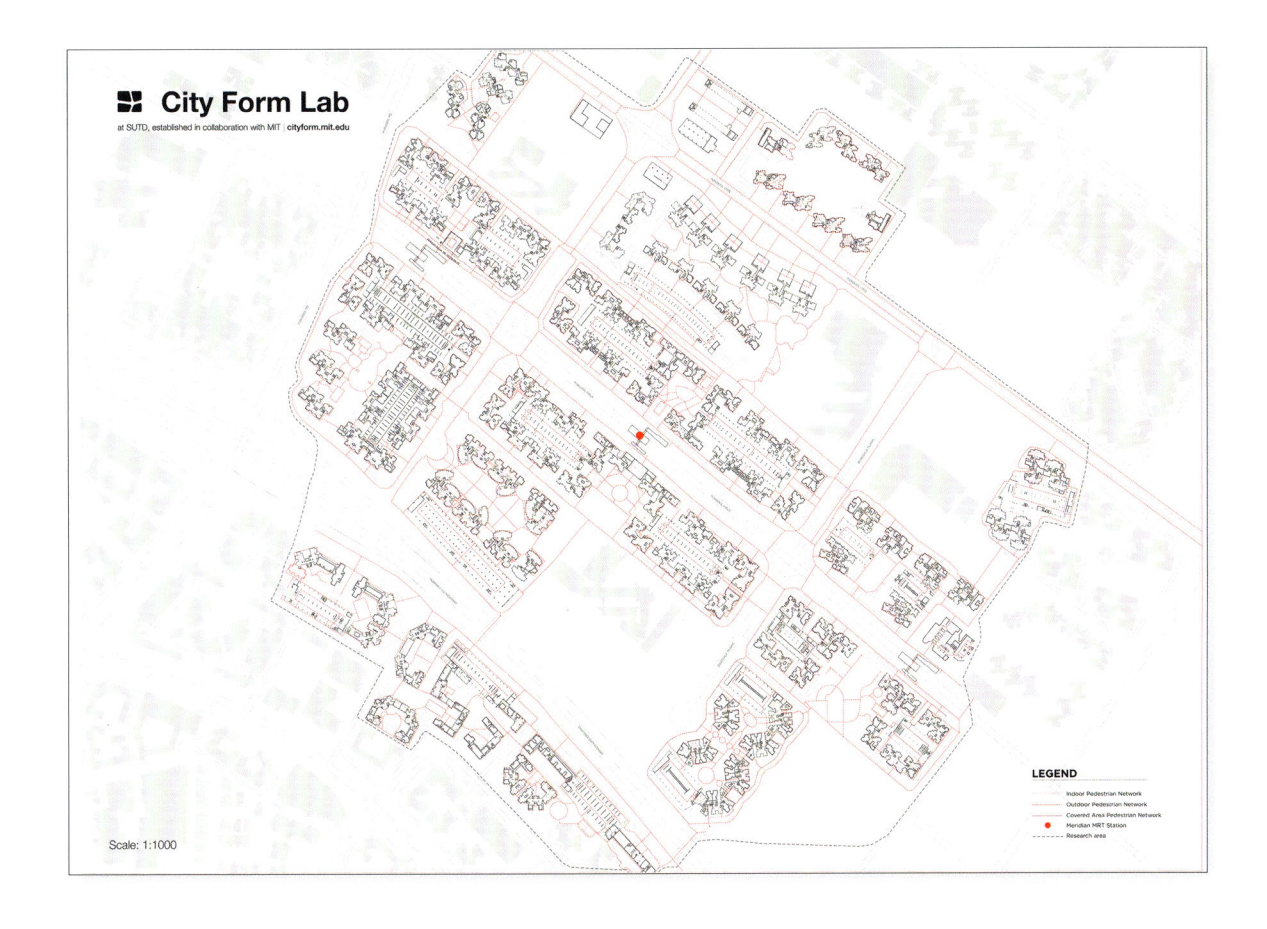

Perkins+Will and AREA Research, the practice's non-profit company specifically set up to support research collaborations between academia and practice, have also created a series of internal research labs organised around lines of enquiry that directly support project execution with parallel research efforts

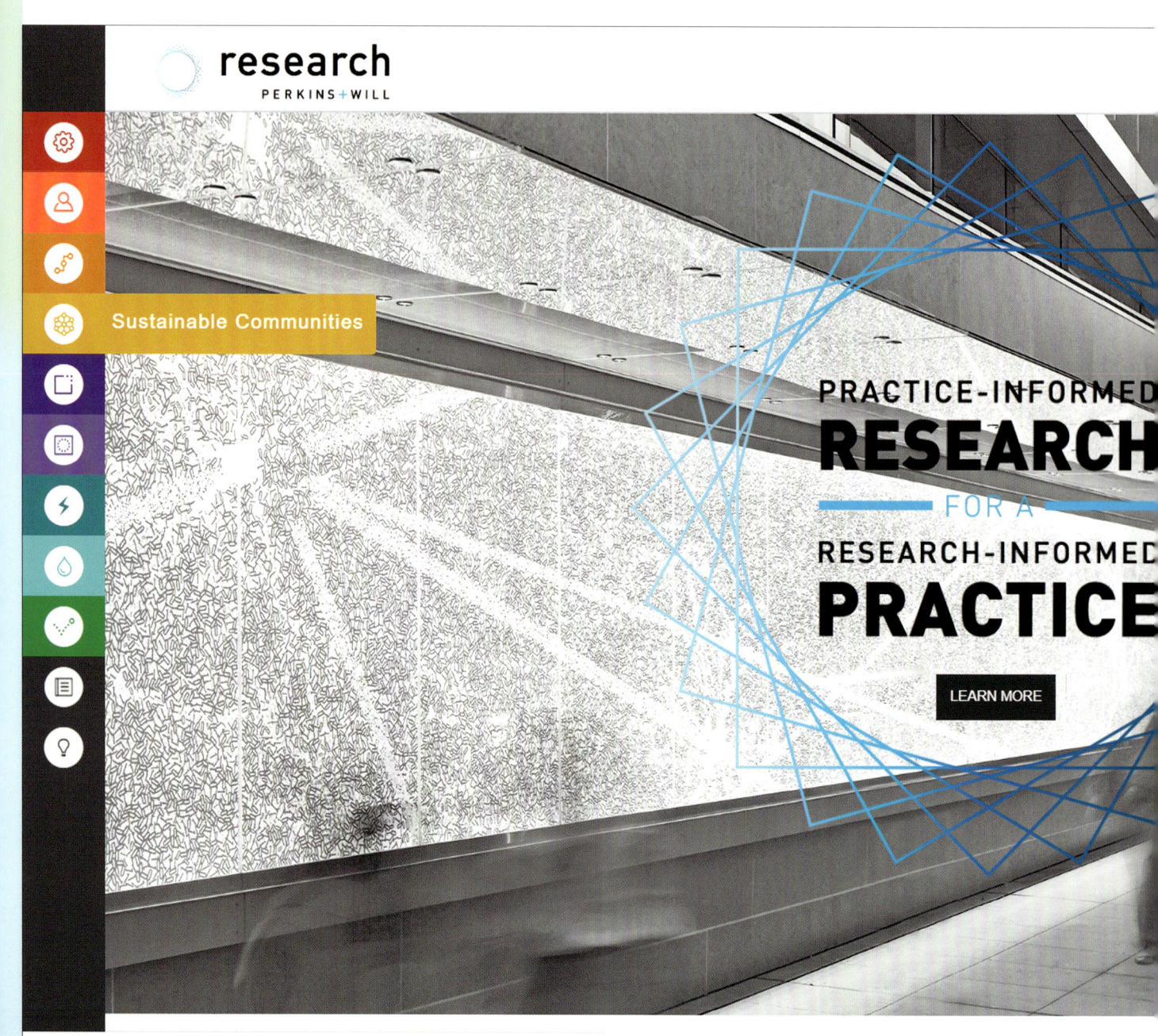

research.perkinswill.com/labs/community/

With these challenges in mind, the City Form Lab, now based at the Harvard University Graduate School of Design but linked to other academic institutions such as the Massachusetts Institute of Technology (MIT) and ETH Zurich, conducts research on urban morphology through spatial analysis and statistics, and creates tools and software to aid the collection and analysis of data. Development partnerships include a number of academic institutions, public entities and private enterprise. In studies such as its Samples of Urban Fabric in Singapore, the Lab has carried out quantitative assessments of the role of urban design and its impact on the quality of life of citizens. The Singapore study relied on a quantitative comparative analysis of areas within a 10-minute walk of a transport station, identifying and comparing physical attributes in three dimensions. Quantifying precisely and comparing what is built is the first step in our understanding of different health and quality-of-life outcomes.

Perkins+Will and AREA Research, the practice's non-profit company specifically set up to support research collaborations between academia and practice, have also created a series of internal research labs organised around lines of enquiry that directly support project execution with parallel research efforts. Separated by a degree from the daily pressures of project deadlines and fees, these research groups are able to delve more deeply into questions that span multiple projects and typologies, for example material performance, sustainability at the district scale, and the human experience of space.

Less Grey, More Black and White

Because of this visible need for more convergence in methodology, I take issue with the findings of the Guest-Editors that the most valuable research in this ⌓ is that which provides a dialogue between different audiences. It may be that the initiatives described in each article were most successful because of this dialogue (although in the spirit of this article, I want to see the supporting evidence), but it is not a measure of success in terms of the research itself. The Guest-Editors also describe how all essays in this issue have recognised their own way of engaging in research to expand its value within practice. But research is not about the individual carving out a unique place in the world; on the contrary, it should be focused on providing results that indicate dispassionate, unbiased findings that add to the body of knowledge of the discipline and can be utilised in this pursuit.

Research may be a grey area for architects, but it needs to be much more black and white. It may be a buzzword in architecture firms, but it is certainly not one in research facilities across the globe. It is the fundamental process of expanding knowledge.

For all the generalisations I have made above, others will certainly provide examples to counter them. In the end, we will never be the scientists who are working to cure cancer or solve our energy needs, but it would be nice if we were at least a profession that understands how our work affects those who live and work in our buildings and our cities. Are we making people healthier and more fulfilled? We simply don't know, and that is our biggest challenge. ⌓

Perkins+Will,
Internal research lab organisation,
2018

The Perkins+Will individual labs provide internal research initiatives to support practical application. These range from detailed technical investigations into materials, to broader-reaching reviews of social sustainability and human experience of space.

Text © 2019 John Wiley & Sons Ltd. Images: p 126 Courtesy of Perkins+Will. © Ben Grubb; pp 127, 130, 132-3 © Perkin+Will, Inc; pp 128-9 Courtesy of Space Syntax; p 131 © City Form Lab, Harvard University. Data collected by SUTD City Form Lab (http://cityform.mit.edu) and distributed under CC BY-SA 3.0 license

CONTRIBUTORS

Jon Ardern is a designer, artist and technologist. As a co-founder and director of Superflux he develops long-term vision and strategy for the studio alongside prototyping and materials investigation. His work has been exhibited at the Museum of Modern Art (MoMA) in New York and Victoria and Albert Museum (V&A) in London, and has won prizes from UNESCO and New York's Social Design Network. He has lectured at the Architectural Association (AA) in London, MAD Faculty at the LUCA School of Arts in Genk, Belgium, and at Kitchen Budapest, Hungary.

Anne Boddington is a Professor of Design Innovation, and Pro Vice Chancellor for Research, Business and Innovation at Kingston University in the UK. Educated as an architect, an urbanist and subsequently as a cultural geographer, she has extensive experience of independent governance and over 30 years' leadership and management experience in higher education, nationally and internationally, spanning teaching, research, business and civic engagement with particular expertise in architecture, art, design and humanities. She is currently Sub Panel Chair for Art and Design: History, Practice and Theory for the UK's Research Excellence Framework (REF) 2021.

Alison Creba has worked in the arts, trades and academia, and recently obtained a Master's in Heritage Conservation from Carleton University in Ottawa, Canada. At the time of this writing, she was embedded at Rotor in Brussels as a resident researcher and restoration technician.

Daniel Davis is a Director of Research at WeWork. Based in New York, he leads a team of researchers investigating how architecture impacts people. The team's work combines data science and social science to better understand how spaces can be designed to enhance people's happiness, productivity and connection to their community. He has a PhD in computational design from RMIT University in Melbourne, Australia. His research at WeWork has appeared in a variety of publications, including *Wired* and *Fast Company*.

Lionel Devlieger obtained his PhD in architectural history and theory from Ghent University in Belgium. In 2005 he co-founded Rotor with Tristan Boniver and Maarten Gielen, where he is now a full-time project manager.

David Green is Principal, Global Practice Leader, Urban Design at Perkins+Will in London, and the current CEO of AREA Research, the non-profit research arm of the company. He received the American Institute of Architects (AIA) Atlanta Silver Medal in 2003 and the AIA Georgia Bronze Medal in 2008. He was a faculty member of the Georgia Institute of Technology College of Architecture in Atlanta from 1992 to 2013 as appointed Professor of the Practice of Architecture, where he taught studios focused on research both at the building level and as urban design studios. He lectures and publishes widely on issues of urban design, planning and architecture.

Jane Hall is a member of multidisciplinary collective Assemble. She studied architecture at the University of Cambridge and the Royal College of Art (RCA) in London, where she received her PhD in 2018. She was the inaugural recipient of the British Council's Lina Bo Bardi Fellowship in 2013, and her subsequent work on public space, occupation and collective action has been published in the *Architectural Review*, *Blueprint* and most recently in *Matzine*.

Harriet Harriss is a qualified architect, a Reader in Architectural Education and leads the Architecture Research Programme at the RCA, where she coordinates the postgraduate research programme in architecture. Her teaching, research and writing largely focus on pioneering new pedagogic models for design education. She is co-editor of the books *Radical Pedagogies: Architectural Education and the British Tradition* (RIBA Publishing, 2015) and *A Gendered Profession: The Question of Representation in Space Making* (RIBA Publishing, 2016). She was awarded a Clore Fellowship (2016–17) and elected to the European Association of Architectural Education Council in 2017. She is also a member of the UK Department for Education construction industry panel.

Martyn Hook is Dean of the School of Architecture and Urban Design at RMIT University and Director of multi-award-winning iredale pedersen hook architects, a studio practice based in Melbourne and Perth dedicated to the appropriate design of effective sustainable buildings with a responsible environmental and social agenda. In balancing these two roles he is a passionate advocate for maintaining a strong and critical relationship between architectural practice and architectural education. He was the Founding Director of the RMIT PhD Programme in Europe, PRS_EU, which gathers a collection of Europe-based practitioners to engage in research through design practice, and oversaw the expansion of this programme in Asia.

Rory Hyde is the Curator of Contemporary Architecture and Urbanism at the V&A, Adjunct Senior Research Fellow at the University of Melbourne, and Design Advocate for the Mayor of London. His writing on architecture and the future of design practice has been featured in the *Economist*, *Guardian*, *Harvard Design Magazine*, *Domus* and *Blueprint*. His book *Future Practice: Conversations from the Edge of Architecture* (Routledge, 2012) was awarded an Australian Institute of Architects prize for architecture in the media.

Anab Jain is a designer, filmmaker, educator and futurist. She co-founded the vanguard laboratory, design and film studio Superflux to parse uncertainties around our shared futures. She is Professor of Design Investigations at the University of Applied Arts, Vienna, and a TED Fellow. Her work has won awards from UNESCO, Apple Inc, the Geneva Human Rights Film Festival and Innovate UK, and has been exhibited at the V&A and Tate Modern in London, MoMA, National Museum of China in Beijing, and the Vitra Design Museum in Weil am Rhein, Germany.

Michael Jones is a senior partner at Foster + Partners who has been with the practice for over 30 years and is now a deputy head of studio overseeing more than 100 architects working on a wide range of international projects. His focus has been on historical buildings and places, preserving them in sensitive yet compelling ways by releasing their potential and enabling a purposeful future. Michael is an active champion of diversity and inclusion, within the architecture profession and beyond, as a means of building enduring and respectful relationships between different cultures. Most recently he has been responsible for the new Stirling Prize-winning European headquarters for Bloomberg in the City of London.

△D | ARCHITECTURAL DESIGN

THE BUSINESS OF RESEARCH

Lara Kinneir is Leader of Urban Studies at the London School of Architecture (LSA), and a director at New London Architecture. Educated in architecture, her work focuses on enabling design and innovation for the betterment of the city. With a multidisciplinary design and strategy background, Lara has worked in architectural and urban design practices, academia, local government and the charity sector for the past 15 years. She coordinates a network on Urban Governance in UN Habitat's Universities Network Initiative, and is currently completing a PhD entitled 'Enabling the Practice of Design within the Governance of the City'.

Danielle Knight is a futures researcher, digital anthropologist and producer, and a researcher and project manager at Superflux. Her main research interest is the evolution of the concept of 'homo faber': human beings as makers and users of objects. This includes investigating how emerging relationships between human beings and increasingly 'intelligent' nonhuman things might shape the material and digital worlds, our place within them, and our interactions with one another.

Carol Patterson is a director at OMA. During her 18 years at OMA and preceding 10 years as a New York architect, she has managed the complexity of historical preservation, political turf wars, and challenging logistics. She first joined OMA in 2000 to help design the Seattle Public Library. Large-scale projects in the UK include the headquarters for Rothschild in the City of London and the Commonwealth Institute. Current projects include Factory, a new performing arts centre in Manchester, and a sports and science building for Brighton College.

Leon van Schaik is Emeritus Professor at the School of Architecture and Urban Design, RMIT University. He has written books on spatial thinking, the poetics of architecture and the processes involved in procuring innovative architecture. The practice-based research PhD programme he initiated has become a template for institutions worldwide. His support of local architectural cultures and his leadership in the procurement of exemplary architecture has resulted in some of Melbourne's most distinguished contemporary buildings. He is a founding member of the Academic Court of the LSA.

James Soane is an architect and teacher. He set up Project Orange with his partner in 1997. The studio is research-led with a diverse range of approaches. He is Director of Critical Practice at the LSA, and a co-editor of the book *A Gendered Profession: The Question of Representation in Space Making* (RIBA Publishing, 2016).

Ziona Strelitz was educated as a social anthropologist, town planner and interior designer, and is a practising researcher, strategist and Founding Director of ZZA Responsive User Environments, where she works with leading clients to shape relevant, boundary-stretching projects. She has judged many awards, been an expert on public panels, and is an author, lecturer and international presenter. Her publications include *Buildings that Feel Good* (RIBA Publishing, 2008) and *Energy People Place: Sustainable Urban Paradigm* (SHP, 2012).

Frederik Weissenborn is Research and Communications Manager of Public Practice, where he oversees – among other things – the Research & Development programme. Prior to joining Public Practice he was in academia for a number of years, conducting research into the relationship between urban form and urban social justice. He also has prior experience working with research and development in the private sector.

John Zhang is an academic and a practising architect. Prior to setting up his own studio he was an associate at DSDHA. He has recently completed a PhD at the RCA, on the subject of the changing relationship between foreign and Chinese architects in contemporary China. He teaches at the School of Architecture and Cities, University of Westminster, where he runs a studio exploring comparative urban morphologies between China and the UK, in collaboration with the Central Academy of Fine Arts in Beijing.

What is *Architectural Design*?

Founded in 1930, *Architectural Design* (△) is an influential and prestigious publication. It combines the currency and topicality of a newsstand journal with the rigour and production qualities of a book. With an almost unrivalled reputation worldwide, it is consistently at the forefront of cultural thought and design.

Each title of △ is edited by an invited Guest-Editor, who is an international expert in the field. Renowned for being at the leading edge of design and new technologies, △ also covers themes as diverse as architectural history, the environment, interior design, landscape architecture and urban design.

Provocative and pioneering, △ inspires theoretical, creative and technological advances. It questions the outcome of technical innovations as well as the far-reaching social, cultural and environmental challenges that present themselves today.

For further information on △, subscriptions and purchasing single issues see:

http://onlinelibrary.wiley.com/journal/10.1002/%28ISSN%291554-2769

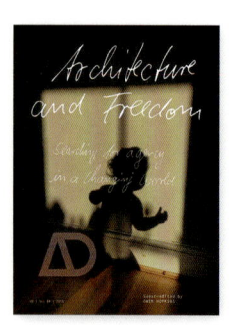

Volume 88 No 3
ISBN 978 1119 332633

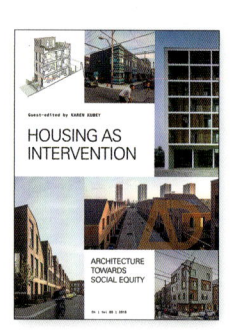

Volume 88 No 4
ISBN 978 1119 337843

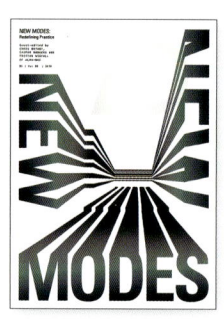

Volume 88 No 5
ISBN 978 1119 328148

Volume 88 No 6
ISBN 978 1119 375951

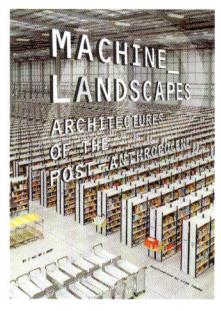

Volume 89 No 1
ISBN 978 1119 453017

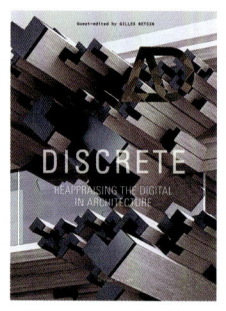

Volume 89 No 2
ISBN 978 1119 500346

Individual backlist issues of △ are available as books for purchase starting at £29.99 / US$45.00

www.wiley.com

How to Subscribe
With 6 issues a year, you can subscribe to △ (either print, online or through the △ App for iPad)

Institutional subscription
£310 / $580
print or online

Institutional subscription
£388 / $725
combined print and online

Personal-rate subscription
£136 / $215
print and iPad access

Student-rate subscription
£90 / $137
print only

△ App for iPad
6-issue subscription:
£44.99 / US$64.99
Individual issue:
£9.99 / US$13.99

To subscribe to print or online
E: cs-journals@wiley.com

Americas
E: cs-journals@wiley.com
T: +1 781 388 8598
or +1 800 835 6770
(toll free in the USA & Canada)

Europe, Middle East and Africa
E: cs-journals@wiley.com
T: +44 (0) 1865 778315

Asia Pacific
E: cs-journals@wiley.com
T: +65 6511 8000

Japan (for Japanese-speaking support)
E: cs-japan@wiley.com
T: +65 6511 8010
or 005 316 50 480
(toll-free)

Visit our Online Customer Help available in 7 languages at www.wileycustomerhelp.com/ask

NOW available on the iPad!

- Buy single issues or subscribe
- Store all downloaded issues to your personal library
- Easily navigable format brings new life to △ articles
- Free to personal print subscribers